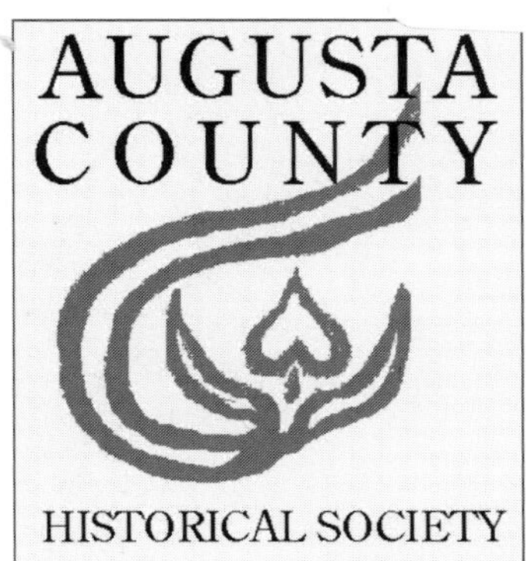

The Augusta County Historical Society
joins with Robert H. Moore II in bringing to the public

GIBRALTAR OF THE SHENANDOAH

Civil War Sites and Stories of Staunton, Waynesboro, and Augusta County, Virginia

another volume of the Society's publications
presenting the rich history of Augusta County.

Augusta County Historical Society was founded in 1964.

The mission of the Augusta County Historical Society is to study, collect, preserve, publish, and promote the history of Augusta County and its communities. The Society also strives to make the citizens of Augusta County aware of their heritage.

Augusta County Historical Society
Post Office Box 686
Staunton, VA 24402-0686

www.augustacountyhs.org

THE
DONNING COMPANY
PUBLISHERS

GIBRALTAR OF THE SHENANDOAH

Civil War Sites and Stories of Staunton, Waynesboro, and Augusta County, Virginia

Robert H. Moore II

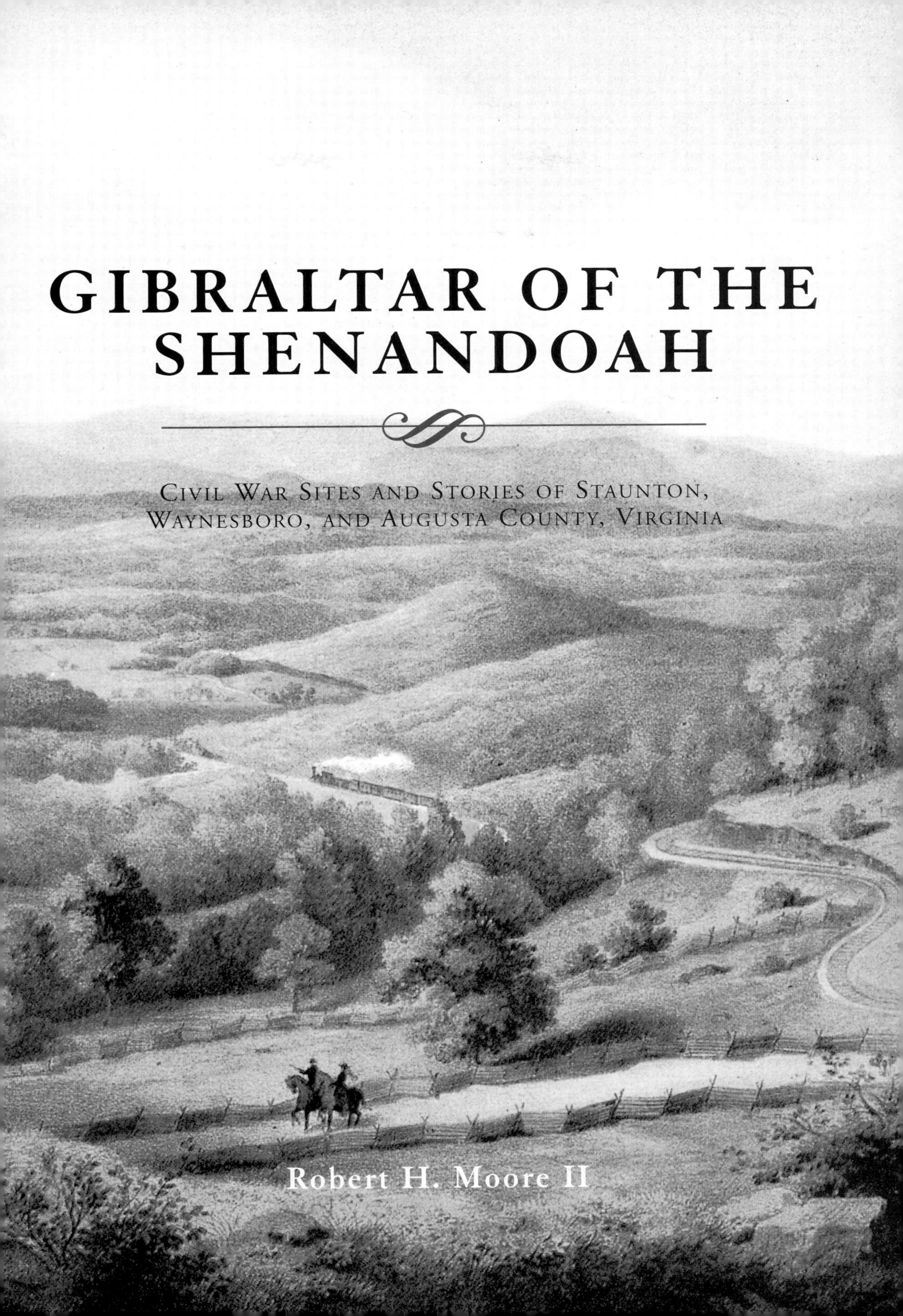

THE DONNING COMPANY PUBLISHERS
184 Business Park Drive, Suite 206
Virginia Beach, VA 23462

Steve Mull, *General Manager*
Barbara B. Buchanan, *Office Manager*
Anne Cordray, *Project Research Coordinator*
Richard A. Horwege, *Senior Editor*
Andrea L. W. Eisenberger, *Graphic Designer*
Mary Ellen Wheeler, *Proofreader/Editorial Assistant*
Stephanie Danko, *Imaging Artist*
Scott Rule, *Director of Marketing*
Travis Gallup, *Marketing Coordinator*

Dennis N. Walton, *Project Director*

Library of Congress Cataloging-In-Publication Data

Moore, Robert H.

Gibraltar of the Shenandoah : Civil War sites and stories of Staunton, Waynesboro, and Augusta County, Virginia / by Robert H. Moore II.
p. cm.
Includes bibliographical references and index.
ISBN 1-57864-266-3 (soft cover : alk. paper)

1. Historic sites—Virginia—Staunton—Guidebooks. 2. Historic sites— Virginia—Waynesboro—Guidebooks. 3. Historic sites—Virginia—Augusta County— Guidebooks. 4. Staunton (Va.)—Tours. 5. Waynesboro (Va.)—Tours. 6. Augusta County (Va.)—Tours. 7. Shenandoah River Valley (Va. and W. Va.)—History—Civil War, 1861–1865—Antiquities. 8. United States—History—Civil War, 1861–1865— Antiquities. I. Title.
F234.S8M66 2004
973.7'3'0975591—dc22

2004013143

Printed in the United States of America
by Walsworth Publishing Company

To my wife,
Danette

Table of Contents

IS A TRUE GLORY AND A TRUE
OF DUTY DONE.

Acknowledgments

First and foremost, thanks go to my wife and children for their patience while "Daddy" typed away at the keyboard. Without their support, this book would most certainly not have been possible.

Thanks are also extended to Donning Company Publishers, an organization that has set up this very unique system that is designed to benefit nonprofit entities. Dennis Walton, Richard Horwege, and Andrea Eisenberger have been wonderful throughout.

Thanks to the Augusta County Historical Society for giving sponsorship for the book. May they direct a significant portion of the funds raised from this book toward the very sites that are mentioned in this book, either through interpretive aids or preservation.

Thanks also to many different folks, institutions and organizations for materials, photos, information, and assistance including Madison and Katharine Brown, Ms. Kendrick Brown, Rick Chittum, Mrs. Nelda Epps, Richard M. Hamrick Jr., John L. Heatwole, Howard Kittell and the Shenandoah Valley Battlefields Foundation, Ken Koons, Rod McDonnell, Nancy Sorrells, the Augusta Military Academy Museum, the Hagley Museum and Library, the Hanger Orthopedic Group, the Library of Congress, the Library of Virginia, the Mason and Hanger-Silas Mason Company, the National Archives, the Staunton Military Academy Alumni Association and Museum, the United States Army Military History Institute, the University of Virginia, Washington and Lee University, the Waynesboro Heritage Foundation, Inc., and the West Virginia Division of Culture and History.

In many ways, the inspiration for this book, along with the first one in this series about Page County sites, has come through my affiliation with Virginia Civil War Trails. Mitch Bowman, the Executive Director, has been a great help in seeing that many of the obscure sites throughout Virginia have received proper interpretation. Additionally, thanks are extended to Bil Cullen of Communication Design, who was responsible for designing the maps in this book. I also thank God for seeing me through such a wonderful project.

Introduction and a Note to the Reader

This book consists of a nearly 500-mile, 104-stop/86-site tour of places and buildings throughout Staunton, Waynesboro, and Augusta County that were impacted in a particular way during the American Civil War. However, understanding time constraints, the tours are broken into eleven different chapters/tours that allow you to pick and choose which one or more are right for you at a particular time. You have the option to follow the tours as they are written, or create your own by using the numbering system of the individual sites.

Please remember to be particularly safe and adhere to posted speed limits. Additionally, make certain that when you do read the book while on the driving tour, you do so only after you have made a complete stop in an area that will give you time and safety to read the information about the particular site at which you have stopped. As you drive from site to site there are also some other things to keep in mind:

1) Unless it is indicated in the text that you may enter a property or house for an additional touring experience, and since most of the properties/houses are privately owned, please respect private property.

2) There are stops at active churches. Please respect their privacy during services.

3) There are stops that offer walks through cemeteries. Please be considerate during funeral services.

4) Use caution on the approach to and at some stops. You will be leaving hard surfaced roads to enter gravel or dirt lanes that are sometimes narrow and can be dangerous if excessive speed is taken. It is best to remain under thirty miles per hour on most of the gravel roads.

5) Unless you stop in a recommended parking area at or near a stop, it is recommended that you turn on your hazard lights.

6) Enjoy Staunton, Waynesboro, and Augusta County's Civil War sites!

As the southern entrance point of the Shenandoah Valley, Augusta County offers great venues for interpreting the Civil War in the Shenandoah Valley. In addition to claiming its own sites and battlefields, Augusta is also a great launch point for tours to the battlefields of McDowell, Cross Keys, Port Republic, and New Market. Just to the south in Lexington, additional Civil War sites are easily accessible via Rt. 11 or Interstate 81.

TOUR NO. 1 1861, SECESSION AND MOBILIZATION

BEGIN TOUR NO. 1 AT THE AMERICAN FARM at the Frontier Culture Museum (Stop No. 1) in Staunton. Refer to the maps on pages 122–125 for assistance in locating the sites on this tour. This tour is approximately 67 miles in length and includes 18 stops at historic buildings and sites.

STOP NO. 1 AMERICAN FARM, FRONTIER CULTURE MUSEUM OF VIRGINIA

Though the museum's Barger Farm was originally relocated from Botetourt County, the house, barn, and accompanying buildings exhibit an excellent example of agrarian lifestyles in Augusta County before the Civil War. The architectural styles and physical layout of these buildings show English, German, and Scots-Irish cultural influence. These three cultural groups migrated into the Valley and settled here in large numbers during the eighteenth century.

By 1860, Augusta County, like all counties of the Shenandoah Valley, featured a well-established agrarian economy. High levels of grain production in the region led to its wide renown as the "Breadbasket of the Confederacy." With 1,552 farms covering over 225,000 acres of

The Barger Farm at the Frontier Culture Museum.

improved land, Augusta County was second only to Rockingham County in agricultural production. Many Augusta County farms incorporated the use of slave labor. In fact, with over 5,600 slaves among 811 slaveholders (about 20 percent of the overall population), Augusta County's slave population was among the highest in the Shenandoah Valley.

With an effective turnpike system, a railroad, the Shenandoah River, and access to the James River canal system to the south, the farmers of Augusta County, and the farmers of most of the southern and central Shenandoah Valley, enjoyed excellent access to transportation arteries that allowed distribution of their products to a wide range of markets to the east, across the Blue Ridge.

During the Civil War, the transportation system that had served Augusta County's farmers so well, especially the Virginia Central Railroad, proved critical to the efforts of the Confederate high command in maintaining control of this vital region of Virginia. The rail lines running to Staunton would make the town a primary objective of Federal armies seeking to shut down Confederate activities in the Shenandoah Valley.

From the Frontier Culture Museum, proceed down Cochran Parkway .9 miles. Turn left on Richmond Road/Rt. 250 West and proceed 1.8 miles and merge right under railroad underpass and continue left on Greenville Avenue for .2 miles. The modern courthouse stands on the site of the old courthouse at the corner of Johnson and Augusta Streets.

Old Augusta County Court House — Stop No. 2

During the 1860 presidential election, Constitutional Union Party Candidate John Bell carried Augusta County with 2,553 votes, followed by Northern Democrat Candidate Stephen A. Douglas with 1,094, and Southern Democrat Candidate John C. Breckinridge with 218 votes. Though Virginia, Kentucky, and Tennessee supported Bell and Missouri went to Douglas, most of the South stood behind Breckinridge. In the end, however, Abraham Lincoln won the overall popular vote in the United States, triggering the states of the Deep South to move immediately toward secession.

Augusta County Court House, circa 1890.
From *Staunton: The Queen City*

By February, the tone of the pro-Union stand in Augusta County was clear; three of the elected delegates to the Virginia Convention were all conservative Unionists. Delegates Alexander H. H. Stuart, George Baylor, and John B. Baldwin were all dedicated to the preservation of the Union and stood firm against the secession movement.

Though the initial vote on April 4 indicated Virginia's opposition to secession, in the vote on

Seal of the Commonwealth of Virginia at the time of the war.

April 17, two days after Lincoln's call for troops, the Commonwealth shifted in both attitude and votes, passing the Ordinance of Secession. Three days later the *Staunton Spectator* praised the "steadfast efforts of Virginia to negotiate a settlement in the Union. However, now that Lincoln has issued a call for troops and peace has failed, it has become appropriate for Virginians to abandon their quest for peace and fight for the Commonwealth." On May 7, 1861, Virginia became the eighth state to join the Confederacy. On May 23, 1861, public support for secession was measured through a referendum vote. In Augusta County the vote tallied 3,130 in favor and 10 against. Within days, local troops began mustering into the service of the Confederacy, marching from Staunton and Waynesboro to Harpers Ferry.

From the courthouse, the John B. Baldwin House once stood on Augusta Street, just behind the county courthouse. Baldwin later lived in "Hessian House" where the playground in Gypsy Hill Park presently stands.

Stop No. 3

Site of the John Brown Baldwin House

John Brown Baldwin.
From *Beautiful Thornrose Cemetery*, 1907

By the time of the Secession Convention, John Brown Baldwin, a prominent Augusta County lawyer, already had an extensive career in law and politics. Following the election of Lincoln, Baldwin was one of Augusta County's three elected representatives to Virginia's Secession Convention.

One of the most intriguing aspects of Baldwin's involvement in the secession process was his participation in the Virginia Unionist movement to prevent war. On April 4, Baldwin, selected by his fellow Unionists to meet with President Lincoln, presented the argument to Lincoln that if he were to uphold the Constitution "without regard to party or section"; reject the right of secession but grant the Confederacy de facto recognition; call a national convention of the states; and withdraw Federal troops from Forts Sumter and Pickens, he might discover that "there is national feeling enough in the seceded States themselves and all over the country to rally to your support." Little is known of the impact of Baldwin's pleas upon Lincoln, but Baldwin did make it clear that South Carolina was in the act of "asserting a right" and that if shots were fired in Charleston Harbor "from whichever side, Virginia herself will be out [of the Union] in forty-eight hours. If there is a gun fired at Sumter, this thing is gone."

As a Virginian, Baldwin, despite his early opposition to secession, held firm to the support of his state's decision for war. Within four months of his meeting with Lincoln, Baldwin was appointed colonel of the 52nd Virginia Infantry. Before the end of the war he would also serve as a member of the Confederate Congress and as colonel of the Augusta Reserves and Raid Guard. After the war he served as a member of the "Committee of Nine," which facilitated the adoption of a state constitution and reentrance of Virginia to the Union in 1870. Baldwin died in 1873 and was buried in Thornrose Cemetery.

From the Baldwin House site, continue .1 miles and turn left on E. Frederick. Proceed .1 miles and turn left on Lewis Street. Proceed .15 miles and turn right on W. Johnson Street. Continue approximately .1 miles to Church Street and turn left. The Stuart House is .05 miles on the right.

Alexander Hugh Holmes Stuart House

Stop No. 4

120 Church Street
(circa 1791)

By the time of the Secession Convention, Alexander H. H. Stuart, a brother-in-law of J. B. Baldwin, had also enjoyed an extensive career as a lawyer and politician—serving as a member of the United States Congress and as secretary of the interior in the cabinet of President Millard Fillmore. An old-line Whig, Stuart opposed secession to the utmost of his ability. Although he had led several Union meetings in Augusta County, in the end Stuart did not approve of the use of military force against the seceded states, and so he voted for secession.

Following Baldwin's return from the Lincoln conference, Stuart, as a part of an official three-member delegation, went to meet Lincoln to reinforce Baldwin's pleas and seek solid reassurances from Lincoln that he would not attack the South. A severe storm washed out the roads and delayed his arrival in Washington until April 12. By the time of their arrival at Lincoln's office, the first shots had already been fired on Sumter, and Lincoln made it clear that he would "repel force by force." Nevertheless, Stuart continued to appeal to Lincoln, and even after the interview he believed that Lincoln's words did not indicate the onset of a "general war." However, on the following day, Richmond newspapers printed Lincoln's Proclamation calling for seventy-five thousand troops that, Virginians believed, would be used to coerce the seceded states.

Alexander H. H. Stuart.
FROM *ALEXANDER HUGH HOLMES STUART*, 1925

Alexander H. H. Stuart House

From the Stuart House, continue along Church Street for .1 miles and turn left on Middlebrook Avenue. Proceed .1 miles and turn left on S. Lewis. Proceed for .1 miles and turn right on W. Johnson Street. Continue .35 miles and turn left on N. Coalter Street. The Wilson House will be approximately .25 miles on left near corner of Coalter and Frederick.

Following the war, Stuart returned to politics and, in 1868, became the chairman of the "Committee of Nine," which was instrumental in restoring Virginia to the Union. Stuart died in 1891 and was buried in Thornrose Cemetery.

Stop No. 5

24 North Coalter Street

Joseph Ruggles Wilson Residence/ Woodrow Wilson Birthplace

Born in Steubenville, Ohio, in 1822, Joseph Ruggles Wilson was not only known as the father of President Woodrow Wilson, but also for his role in history as a prominent Presbyterian clergyman and professor. Although Joseph Wilson had been reared in Ohio, after moving to Virginia and becoming the pastor of Staunton's Presbyterian Church, he became "unreconstructedly Southern" in values and politics. Wilson and his family resided here at the Presbyterian Manse.

Moving to Augusta, Georgia, before the Civil War, Wilson continued in his role as a Presbyterian minister. There, his "Mutual Relation of Masters and Slaves as Taught in the Bible" sermon of January 6, 1861, at the First Presbyterian Church in Augusta, Georgia, displayed his attitude and drew a great deal of interest. When asked to submit his sermon for publication two days later, Wilson responded, "It is surely high time that the Bible view of slavery should be examined, and that we should begin to meet the infidel fanaticism of our infatuated enemies upon the elevated ground of a divine warrant for the institution we are resolved to cherish." By December 1861, Wilson was directly involved in establishing the Confederate or Southern Presbyterian Church.

Dr. Joseph R. Wilson and his wife, Jessie Woodrow.
FROM *STAUNTON, VIRGINIA: A PICTORIAL HISTORY*

As young Thomas Woodrow Wilson grew up, Joseph continued to teach his son about the justification for Southern secession. Interestingly, on June 4, 1914, as president of the United States, Woodrow Wilson took part in the dedication of the Confederate Monument in the Confederate section of Arlington National Cemetery. Among a crowd of thousands, including Confederate and Union veterans, Wilson accepted the monument on behalf of the nation. President Wilson said, "I am not so much happy as proud to participate in this capacity on such an occasion; proud that I should represent such a people."

Joseph R. Wilson Residence/ Woodrow Wilson Birthplace.

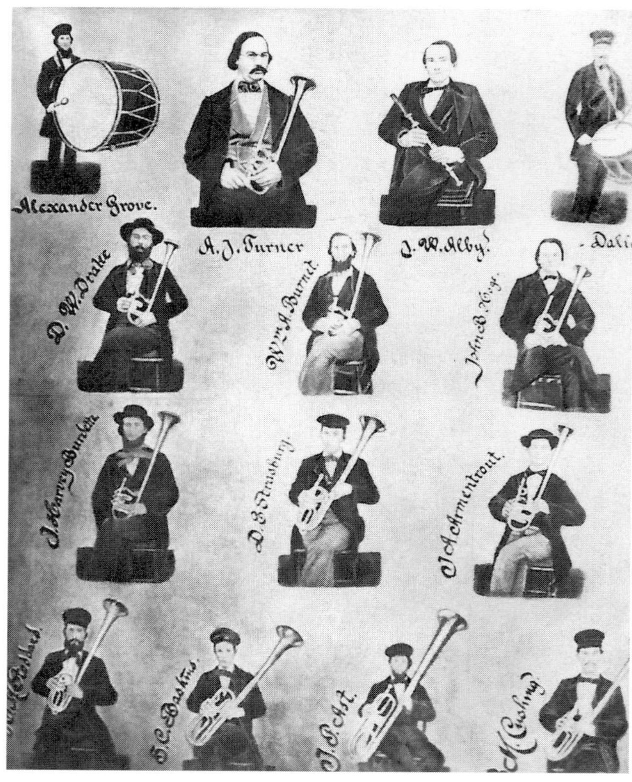

Many of the prewar band members seen in this photo also saw service as members of the Stonewall Brigade Band during the Civil War.
From the Hamrick Collection

From the Wilson House, proceed .13 miles along E. Frederick and turn left on Central Street. Continue approximately .05 miles and turn left on Beverley Street. Though no longer standing, the site of Wayt's Drug Store is on the right at 22 W. Beverley Street.

Stop No. 6 — Stonewall Brigade Band Site

22 W. Beverley Street

Stonewall Brigade Band instruments from the Civil War.
From *Staunton: The Queen City*

Though the original structure has long since been replaced, here in a room over the old Wayt's Drug Store in January 1855, a number of local musicians formed into a group known as David W. Drake's Staunton Mountain Sax-Horn Band. At the time, the men who assembled could not imagine the fame that would crown the small group in time. With the advent of the Civil War, at least five members of the band, then known as [Professor Augustus J.] Turner's Silver Cornet Band, enlisted in many of the different companies of the 5th Virginia Infantry. The first member of the band to fall in the conflict was William E. Woodward at the First Battle of Manassas on July 21, 1861; his last words being "I'll never retreat! Victory or death."

Throughout the first year of the war, the band members occasionally joined together with other musicians from other regiments to perform. At one point during 1861, the band members of the 5th Regiment serenaded Stonewall Jackson and prompted him to write to his wife: "I wish my darling could be with me now and enjoy the sweet music of the brass band of the Fifth Regiment. It is an excellent Band." In April 1862, the former members of Turner's band became officially known as a band component of the 5th Regiment. In addition to their duties as musicians, the men also were designated as hospital corpsmen, litter bearers, and general assistants at field hospitals.

In December 1862, soon after Christmas, the band members were detailed for picket duty along the Rappahannock River, below Fredericksburg. While watching their posts diligently through the day, at night the band would put aside their Austrian rifles for their musical instruments and exchanged serenades each night with the Federal band across the river. Later that winter, the band was designated the official band of the First Brigade, which would later become known as the Stonewall Brigade, after Jackson's death in May 1863. By the end of the war, many from the band, whose members were, by now, made up of men from throughout the Shenandoah Valley, were present at the surrender at Appomattox in April 1865.

From 22 W. Beverley, continue to Augusta Street and turn right. Continue straight until you reach the railroad depot.

Staunton Depot/ The Staunton Artillery

Stop No. 7A

Coming into existence within the same month as John Brown's capture at Harpers Ferry in 1859, the Staunton Artillery would prove to be one of the finest and most active artillery units in the Army of Northern Virginia in the upcoming war. In the midst of the Secession Convention in April 1861, the artillery battery was also to be used as a pawn in the first actions of the war. John Daniel Imboden, the commander of the battery, along with Oliver R. Funsten, Richard and Turner Ashby, John S. and Alfred Barbour, and John A. Harman, had met with former Governor Henry A. Wise to discuss plans concerning the seizing of the Federal Arsenal at Harpers Ferry. Wise explained that the expedition needed official sanctioning, so three of the members, including Imboden, were asked to meet with Governor John Letcher. Letcher, not willing to "promote any hostile action against the United States without apprising the Convention and conferring with it," declined the offer. When Letcher's reaction was relayed to Wise, the former governor acted on his own and conferred with the men as to how the garrison would be taken.

John D. Imboden.
COURTESY OF THE LIBRARY OF CONGRESS

Henry A. Wise.
FROM *GENERALS IN GRAY*/ WARNER COLLECTION

Having sent ahead a telegram to prepare the militia to be ready to march, when Imboden and Harman arrived in Staunton at 6 p.m. on April 17, they were greeted there by the men of the Staunton Artillery as well as thousands from the town's population to see the men off. At

John Letcher,
wartime governor of Virginia.
FROM LIBRARY OF VIRGINIA

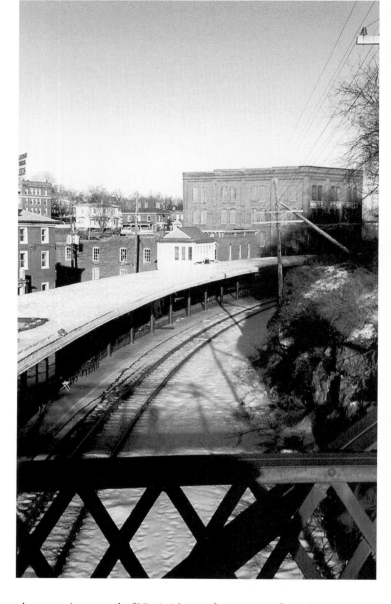

Modern view of the railroad at Staunton Depot from the walking bridge.

From the depot, continue to S. Lewis and turn right. Continue .1 miles and turn right on W. Johnson Street. Continue .35 miles and turn left on N. Coalter Street. Continue .2 miles and turn right on E. Beverley Street. Virginia School for the Deaf and Blind is approximately .22 miles on the right.

the same time, word of Virginia's vote for secession flowed through the local population like an electrical jolt.

Following a number of speeches and prayers, the troops, under General Harman, boarded trains bound for war. When the soldiers arrived at Harpers Ferry in the early morning hours of April 19, they found the Federals had already burned most of the military wares that could have been of use to the new Confederate government of Virginia. Despite the fire, many arms and much manufacturing equipment were saved for use by the Commonwealth.

Grounds of the Virginia School for the Deaf and Blind/52nd Virginia Infantry

Stop No. 8

Shortly after organizing on August 16, 1861, the 52nd Virginia Infantry, composed mainly of men from Augusta, Rockbridge, and Bath Counties, made camp here on the grounds of the former Deaf, Dumb and Blind Institute, which had since been moved to the Staunton Female Academy. Col. John B. Baldwin, commanding the regiment, had only months before seen Lincoln in person with an appeal to stave off war. Michael Garber Harman, a hotel owner and partner with his brothers in a stagecoach business, served as lieutenant colonel of the 52nd Virginia.

The Augusta County companies in this regiment included the Augusta Fencibles (Company A), Waynesboro Guards (Company B), Letcher Guard [Mossy Creek] (Company C), Harper Guard [Mt. Solon] (Company D), Cline's Company [Mt. Solon] (Company F), Veteran Guards [Fishersville] (Company G), Staunton Pioneers (Company H), and the Men of Augusta [Middlebrook and Greenville] (Company I).

Since so many other Augusta County companies had left earlier in April 1861, it was unusual for Staunton to have a regiment composed mostly of locals so late in the year. Rockbridge County native, Lt. William Knick wrote, "Over 100 girls came every evening for the

Head Quarters, Virginia Forces,
STAUNTON, VA.

MEN OF VIRGINIA, TO THE RESCUE!

Your soil has been invaded by your Abolition foes, and we call upon you to rally at once, and drive them back. We want Volunteers to march immediately to Grafton and report for duty. Come one! Come ALL! and render the service due to your State and Country. Fly to arms, and succour your brave brothers who are now in the field.

[illegible]

Action! Action! should be our rallying motto, and the sentiment of Virginia's inspired Orator, "Give me Liberty or give me Death," animate every loyal son of the Old Dominion! Let us drive back the invading foot of a brutal and desperate foe, or leave a record to posterity that we died bravely defending our homes and firesides,—the honor of our wives and daughters,—and the sacred graves of our ancestors!

[Done by Authority.]
M. G. HARMAN, Maj. Commd'g at Staunton.
J. M. HECK, Lt. Col. Va. Vol.
R. E. COWAN, Maj. Va. Vol.

Early Staunton recruiting poster.

1916 photo of the survivors Co. F, 52nd Virginia Infantry. Standing: Pvt. J. M. Fauver, Cpl. Edmond Furr, Cpl. John C. Rutherford, Pvt. William S. Stover, 1st Lt. John A. Fauver. Sitting: Pvt. John S. Sheets, Capt. James Bumgardner Jr., Pvt. Simon W. Wampler.
From *Beautiful Thornrose: Memorial Edition*

Maj. Henry Kyd Douglas.
Courtesy of the Library of Congress

From VSDB, return along E. Beverley Street to N. Coalter Street and turn right. Proceed .1 miles to the corner of Coalter and Frederick and turn left. Proceed .3 miles to corner of Frederick and Lewis. The Bellview House site was near the northwest corner of the intersection.

dress parade." When the regiment finally departed Staunton on September 10, 1861, citizens of Staunton flocked to the roadsides and cheered the men on as they marched off toward Buffalo Gap and eventually the Greenbrier River to join Confederate forces there.

By the time of the surrender at Appomattox Court House, the regiment had been thinned out considerably from casualties, sickness, and desertions. Of the eight officers and fifty-three men of the 52nd present, only fourteen men were armed. Part of the last brigade to lay down arms at Appamatox, the survivors of the 52nd experienced a soldier's tribute as they walked between the lines of the Federal soldiers. Maj. Henry Kyd Douglas, commanding the brigade, recalled that "Someone in the blue line broke the silence and called for three cheers for the last brigade. . . . It was taken up all about him by those who knew what it meant. But for us this soldierly generosity was more than we could bear. Many of the grizzled veterans wept like women, and my own eyes were as blind as my voice was numb. . . . That line of blue broke its respectful silence to pay such tribute . . . to the little line in grey that had fought them to the finish and only surrendered because it was destroyed."

Asylum for the Deaf and Dumb. From *Virginia Illustrated*

Widow Bell House/ "Bellview"

Stop No. 9

As Staunton was a hotbed of activity and daily troop movement since the beginning of the war, the arrival of one "old soldier" did not seem to draw much attention. Having departed from Richmond by train on July 28, 1861, Gen. Robert E. Lee was bound for the mountains of western Virginia to oversee operations in the Cheat Mountain area. Accompanied only by Col. Augustus Washington, Captain Taylor, two of his private black attendants, and his horses, Lee, carrying little baggage, stepped off the train at the Staunton Depot that same evening with no fanfare.

Gen. Robert E. Lee.
Courtesy of the National Archives

What Lee encountered in Staunton horrified him. Gen. Robert S. Garnett's former troops, which had been demoralized by fighting and the loss of their commanding general in the mountains of western Virginia, were filling the streets of the town. As one historian noted, they were "dirty, bloody realities, ragged men, hungry men, the sick and the road-worn. . . . One Georgia Regiment, shattered in the mountains, had straggled back in such utter despair that its bewildered colonel had granted all its men a furlough without consulting his superiors."

Lee is believed to have spent the night in Widow Bell's house before departing for Monterey on horseback the following morning.

Despite what he had seen in Staunton, as he made his way along the Staunton to Parkersburg Turnpike, he recalled the route as being "a part of the road, as far as Buffalo Gap, I passed over in the summer of 1840, on my return to St. Louis . . . I enjoyed the mountains, as I rode along. The views are magnificent—the valleys so beautiful, the scenery so peaceful. What a glorious world Almighty God has given us. How thankless we are, and how we labour to mar his gifts."

Though Lee's subsequent Western Virginia Campaign would prove less than "glorious," it did prove successful in keeping the Federals from Staunton from the summer of 1861 until Gen. Thomas J. Jackson took up the task during the following spring. Jackson may have also stayed here on June 17, 1862, before moving his army east to join Lee, then commanding the Army of Northern Virginia near Richmond.

From the corner of Frederick and Lewis Streets, turn north onto Lewis Street. and continue .2 miles to Pump Street. and turn right. Continue .1 miles to N. Augusta Street and turn left. Proceed for 3 miles (becomes Rt. 11 North) and turn right at the Inn at Old Virginia Bed and Breakfast (1329 Commerce Road). The house is just beyond the railroad underpass.

Stop No. 10

Inn at Old Virginia B & B,
1329 Commerce Road

John A. Harman House/ "Belle Fonte"

John A. Harman.
From the *Augusta Historical Bulletin*

Born near Waynesboro in 1824, John A. Harman had experienced a great deal before the opening of the Civil War. Initially, Harman had served as a "printer's devil" in the offices of the *Staunton Spectator*, learning the art of publishing under Kenton Harper. After serving as editor of the *Lewisburg Observer*, Harman headed to Texas where he remained until the outbreak of the Mexican War. Following service in that war as a member of Ben McCulloch's Texas Rangers, Harman returned to Staunton, eventually purchasing this house.

By April 1861, as the Virginia Secession Convention voted to leave the Union, Harman was serving with Major General Kenton Harper's 5th Militia Division. Of the several regiments in the 5th Division, three were from Augusta County. These were the 32nd, 93rd, and 160th under Colonels Samuel McCune, William S. Sproul, and William Anderson respectively. Following Virginia's vote for secession, Harper's militia seized the Federal arsenal at Harpers Ferry. Though the Federals had already begun to destroy the arsenal, when Harper's militia descended on the quiet riverfront town, they were still able to take important machinery that would be very beneficial to Virginia in the upcoming war.

Within two months of the Confederate seizure of Harpers Ferry, Harman was appointed captain in the quartermaster department by Col. Thomas J. Jackson, the new commander of the garrison. He served in this capacity for the duration of the war, once assuming duties as the quartermaster for the Army of Northern Virginia and later as quartermaster under Gen. Jubal Early in the 1864 Valley Campaign.

Four of Harman's brothers served as Confederate officers in the war including William H. Harman, Michael G. Harman, Asher W. Harman, and Thomas L. Harman. Of the five, two would die: Thomas in 1861 of typhoid and William in 1865 at the Battle of Waynesboro.

From the Harman House, return to Rt. 11 North to Rt. 275 East/ Woodrow Wilson Parkway. Continue on this road (becomes Rt. 254/Hermitage Road) for 11.9 miles and turn right on Hopeman Parkway. Continue for .9 miles and turn left on Main Street. Proceed .7 miles and turn left on W. Broad Street. Proceed .7 miles to Wayne Avenue to corner of Wayne and Ohio. The railroad depot was located just to your front and right.

John Asher Harman House/ "Belle Fonte."

Site of the Waynesboro Depot

Stop No. 11

Though this is a scene of troops on their way to Manassas, similar scenes were likely at the railroad depots at both Waynesboro and Staunton as troops regularly transited through Augusta County in 1861 and 1862.
From *Battles and Leaders of the Civil War*

While Staunton served as the gathering point for many regiments coming into Virginia from throughout the South, troops often passed through Waynesboro en route to Staunton. One soldier passing through Waynesboro would not soon forget the generosity of its residents. Sgt. Joseph M. G. Medlock, a member of Company E, 1st (Ramsey's) Georgia Infantry and former editor of the *Central Georgian*, wrote:

> At Waynesboro, in Augusta County, Va., we found tables spread with an abundance of provisions for every man on board. We all partook freely of the good things set before us, and gave three hearty cheers for Waynesboro—but especially the ladies—bade them farewell, and went on our way rejoicing.

As Medlock's regiment passed Fishersville, "the citizens" having heard "that our regiment was to pass up the evening before, and made great preparations for giving us a supper, but they had mistaken the time and were greatly disappointed. Some of the ladies of that place visited our regiment after we got to Staunton, bringing baskets of provisions along with them. This is emphatically a land of milk and butter, and the milk has flown freely to the weary soldier wherever it was to be had, with a few exceptions."

From the corner of Wayne and Ohio, turn right and proceed .05 miles. Turn right on Mill Street and proceed .05 miles. Turn right on Broad Street and proceed for .1 miles. Turn left on Wayne Avenue and proceed for .1 miles to the northwest corner of Main and Wayne where Fishburne's General Store once stood.

Stop No. 12

Site of Fishburne's General Store

On April 19, 1861, following the secession of Virginia, Waynesboro's first regular army unit was formed under Captain William Patrick. The company would later become Company E of the 1st Virginia Cavalry. The "Valley Rangers" had begun in the winter of 1859 as a local militia unit. Drilling and holding musters near New Hope, the company also held many of its meetings in the old Waynesboro Academy.

On April 19, Patrick's company formed on Main Street and was presented with a Virginia flag made by the ladies of Waynesboro. Elliott Guthrie Fishburne, a private at the time, recalled the exit from the town: "How vividly the scene comes back of our last mustering . . . as we mounted our horses for the last time—of the motherly caress and cautions—the fathers' advice—the sisters' proud smile and the admiring looks of the younger brothers and the servants—and then, the sly embrace of the sweetheart behind the parlor door, when we rushed in to say good by for the twentieth time!" After the presentation of a new flag made by the ladies of Waynesboro, a brief ceremony at the Academy, and a farewell address from Rev. William T. Richardson, the company departed for Harpers Ferry.

Fishburne's Store.
FROM *WAYNESBORO DAYS OF YORE*

Far left: Postwar photo of Elliott G. Fishburne. FROM *CONFEDERATE VETERAN MAGAZINE*

Left: Maj. William Patrick. FROM THE *LAUREL BRIGADE*

After four years of war, when the end became apparent at Appomattox Court House, most of the men of the 1st Virginia evaded the surrender and rode on toward Lynchburg, where the regiment disbanded. Before heading home, "Ellie" Fishburne, who had been present from the earliest days, helped to strip the regiment's Virginia flag from the staff. With Fishburne's help, Color Sgt. James E. Poague then wrapped the flag carefully around his body, concealed it beneath his coat and took it home with him to Lexington. In a reunion in Staunton in 1901, Poague presented the flag to Sgt. Major David W. Drake, the founder of the Staunton Mountain Sax-Horn Band and, briefly, a member of the 5th Virginia Infantry. Drake had transferred to the Valley Rangers in October 1861.

From the corner of Main and Wayne, turn right on Main Street. Proceed for .7 miles and turn left on Rosser Avenue/Rt. 340 South. Proceed for 15 miles to Rt. 11 South and turn left. Greenville is less than a mile from this point.

GREENVILLE: THE AUGUSTA LEE RIFLES AND GEN. ROBERT DOAK LILLEY

STOP NO. 13

Here, on May 20, 1861, Capt. Robert Doak Lilley organized the Augusta Lee Rifles. As the *Spectator* stated, Lilley had proposed to form a battalion in honor of Maj. Gen. Robert E. Lee. "Young men of intelligence of every portion of the county, are most respectfully and cordially invited to join the Battalion." Before departing from Staunton on June 8, the company received a beautiful battleflag with the state seal on one side and "Liberty or Death" on the other. Originally designated as Company C of the 25th Virginia Infantry, when the regiment was reorganized in April 1862, its designation was changed to 2nd Company D. Beginning its battle career at Rich Mountain in less than a month, the regiment would serve under Stonewall Jackson, John Imboden, Jubal Early, and eventually surrendered as a part of Gen. John B. Gordon's corps at Appomattox Court House.

Right: Gen. Robert Doak Lilley.
FROM *BEAUTIFUL THORNROSE: MEMORIAL EDITION*

Far Right: Gen. James A. Walker. In addition to John D. Imboden and Robert D. Lilley, James A. Walker was also a Confederate general who hailed from Augusta County. Born near Piedmont, Walker was best known for his service as sixth commander of the Stonewall Brigade.
COURTESY OF THE NATIONAL ARCHIVES

Captain Lilley, a native of Greenville, was one of the three natives of Augusta County to rise to generalship. Teaching engineering in Charleston, South Carolina, when Fort Sumter was fired upon, Lilley returned to Virginia immediately and organized the Augusta Lee Rifles.

Lilley was cited for bravery on several occasions and was wounded twice by the time he was promoted to brigadier general in the spring of 1864. In July 1864, while on a reconnaissance near Winchester, Lilley was wounded again and fell into enemy hands. Recuperating at a Winchester home, he was liberated within days but lost his right arm to amputation. Lilley kept the limb in a box and eventually was buried with it when he died in 1886. Lilley last commanded all of the reserves of the Valley District at the end of the war. Lilley was buried in Thornrose Cemetery. Two of Lilley's brothers, including Lt. Col. John Doak Lilley, served in the 52nd Virginia Infantry.

From Greenville, proceed north on Rt. 11 for 2.1 miles. Turn left on Rt. 701/Howardsville Road and proceed for 4.1 miles. Turn right on Rt. 252 N/Middlebrook Road. Proceed for 3.9 miles. Turn left on Smoky Row Road/Rt. 709. Proceed for 2.1 miles. Turn right on Rt. 710 and proceed .5 miles. Turn left on Rt. 708/Glebe School Road. Proceed for 1.9 miles. Walnut Grove will be on your right.

Officers of the West Augusta Guard circa 1861. Baylor is standing in the center. James Bumgardner is seated on the left.
FROM *CONFEDERATE VETERAN MAGAZINE*

Jacob Baylor House/ "Walnut Grove"

Stop No. 14

William Smith Hanger Baylor, was the third of three children and the only son of Jacob and Eveline Hanger Evans, was born in 1831, probably in this house. A graduate of Washington College and a student at the University of Virginia, Baylor was a very personable and popular young man. By 1857, he was Staunton's commonwealth's attorney. In March 1859, Baylor participated in the organization of a local militia force and was elected colonel. However, due to organizational criteria, he was eventually given a lesser position as company commander of the West Augusta Guard.

W. S. H. Baylor.
Courtesy of the Library of Virginia

In the spring of 1861, Baylor was again appointed colonel at the head of several companies from Augusta County. However, after arriving at Harpers Ferry, the militia regiment was reorganized and, again, Baylor was lowered to a lesser rank as major while Kenton Harper held the post of colonel of the regiment. By the spring of 1862, the 5th Virginia Infantry was reorganized and Baylor was appointed colonel. Cited for gallantry in battle on numerous occasions, by August 1862, Baylor was in command of the famous Stonewall Brigade.

On August 30, 1862, during the Battle of Second Manassas and in the heat of the fight against the Federal attack on the unfinished railroad, Baylor saw the color bearer of the 33rd Virginia fall mortally wounded. Rushing to take up the flag and waving it high above him, Baylor yelled, "Boys, follow me!" As the Stonewall Brigade leapt forward in a successful counterattack, Baylor was instantly the target of a Federal volley that literally lifted him off the ground. In line for a commission as a brigadier general, Baylor was the fourth commander of the famed brigade. James A. Walker, another Augusta County native, later became the sixth commander of the brigade.

From Walnut Grove, continue on Rt. 708 for .9 miles. Turn right on Rt. 876. Proceed to Hewitt Road/Rt. 703 and turn right. Continue to Rt. 876/Swoope Road and turn left. Continue 1.6 miles to Rt. 254 West/Parkersburg Turnpike and turn left. Proceed for .3 miles. Idle Wilde will be on a hill on the right.

The Wilson House/"Idle Wilde"/ 5th Virginia Infantry

Stop No. 15

Dating to the mid-nineteenth century, "Idle Wilde" was home to the Wilson family. The Wilsons contributed six sons to the Confederate cause, including five sons who served with the Churchville Cavalry and one who served with the West View Infantry. Remarkably, only one of the young men died in the war. James Brown Wilson was killed at the Battle of Rich Mountain on July 11, 1861. James' body was not found until a hunter discovered it years after the fight.

The Wilson House/"Idle Wilde."

Peter Eidson Wilson was the only son who served in the West View Infantry of the 5th Virginia Regiment. Beginning the war as a 2nd lieutenant, four years later, at Appomattox Court House, as a captain, he surrendered what remained of the "Fighting Fifth" as they marched to the surrender field with the shattered remnants of the Stonewall Brigade.

The 5th Virginia Infantry was composed mainly of Augusta County men. Of all the companies, nine were originally recruited in the county. The companies were organized from their respective communities: Company C, "Mountain Guard" (Spring Hill); Company D, "Southern Guard" (Middlebrook); Company E, "Augusta Greys" (Greenville); Company F, "West View Infantry" (West View and Valley Mills); Company G, "Staunton Rifles" (Staunton); Company H, "Augusta Rifles" (Fishersville); Company I, "Ready Rifles of Augusta County" (Sangerville); Company L, "West Augusta Guard" (Staunton); Company M, "Union Greys"/later "Southern Greys" (Mt. Sidney). Additionally, the future Stonewall Brigade Band included several members from Augusta County.

From Idle Wilde, continue 2.4 miles west on Rt. 254/Parkersburg Turnpike. Turn right on Rt. 42. Proceed for 5.3 miles to Churchville and turn right on Rt. 250 East/Churchville Avenue. Proceed .15 miles and turn left on Rt. 835/Hotchkiss Road. The Hotchkiss House is .3 miles on the left.

From the time they were placed under the command of Gen. Thomas J. Jackson as a part of the 1st Brigade, the 5th Virginia, along with the 2nd, 4th, 27th, and 33rd Virginia Infantries, was, from the Battle of First Manassas, known as the immortal "Stonewall Brigade."

JEDEDIAH HOTCHKISS HOUSE/ "LOCH WILLOW"

STOP NO. 16

Born on November 30, 1828, Jedediah Hotchkiss was a native of Broome County, New York. A budding geologist who found fascination in walking tours of different locales, by the later 1840s he found himself in the Shenandoah Valley and soon called the area his new home. Through a chance meeting with one Henry Forrer in Page County, Virginia, Hotchkiss was offered the opportunity to serve Forrer's brother, Daniel, at Mossy Creek in Augusta County, as a private teacher. In time, the young Hotchkiss' private tutoring led to the establishment of the Mossy Creek Academy, for which he served as principal.

Jedediah Hotchkiss.
FROM *STONEWALL JACKSON'S WAY*

By 1861, Hotchkiss, now married with a child, was operating Loch Willow Academy at Churchville. With the coming of the war and holding firm to his new Virginia identity, Hotchkiss wrote: "All we ask of the North is to be left alone in the enjoyment of our inherited rights." As many of his schoolboys flocked to enlist in the army, Hotchkiss was forced to suspend classes, and volunteered his services to the Confederacy as well. Though his early career with the Confederacy was often uncertain, Hotchkiss began to make a name for himself as a mapmaker. In March 1862, William S. H. Baylor, a friend of Hotchkiss' who served on the staff of Maj. Gen. Thomas J. Jackson, encouraged Hotchkiss to tender his services to Jackson directly. On March 26, 1862, Hotchkiss received word to report to Jackson. "I want you to make me a map of the Valley," spoke Jackson,

Daniel Forrer
FROM *CHRISTIAN FORRER: THE CLOCKMAKER*

Prewar and wartime house of Jedediah Hotchkiss and his family.

From the Hotchkiss House, return to Churchville and proceed approximately .2 miles and turn right into the side driveway of St. James Church.

"from Harpers Ferry to Lexington, showing all the points of offence and defence in those places. Mr. Pendleton will give you orders for whatever outfit you want. Good morning, Sir." Thus the legendary story of Jackson's mapmaker began.

Stop No. 17

St. James Church

Pvt. Abner A. Arnold, Company A, 14th Virginia Cavalry.
From *Staunton: The Queen City*

On May 13, 1861, the Churchville Cavalry was organized here, eventually becoming Company I, 14th Virginia Cavalry. One other company of the 14th Virginia, the "Valley Cavalry" or "Rangers," was organized in May 1862 and was composed of men from southern Augusta County, and Rockbridge and Bath Counties. It became Company C of the 14th.

Initially under the command of Capt. Frank Sterrett, former colonel of the 160th Virginia Militia, the Churchville Cavalry included a number of recruits from the Pastures District of Augusta County, and several were from Hotchkiss' Loch Willow Academy. When the recruits numbered about sixty men, they were enrolled and sworn into service here in the yard of the St. James Church. Most of the men brought their own horses into the service and had to wait for uniforms that were produced at the Odd Fellows Hall under the supervision of

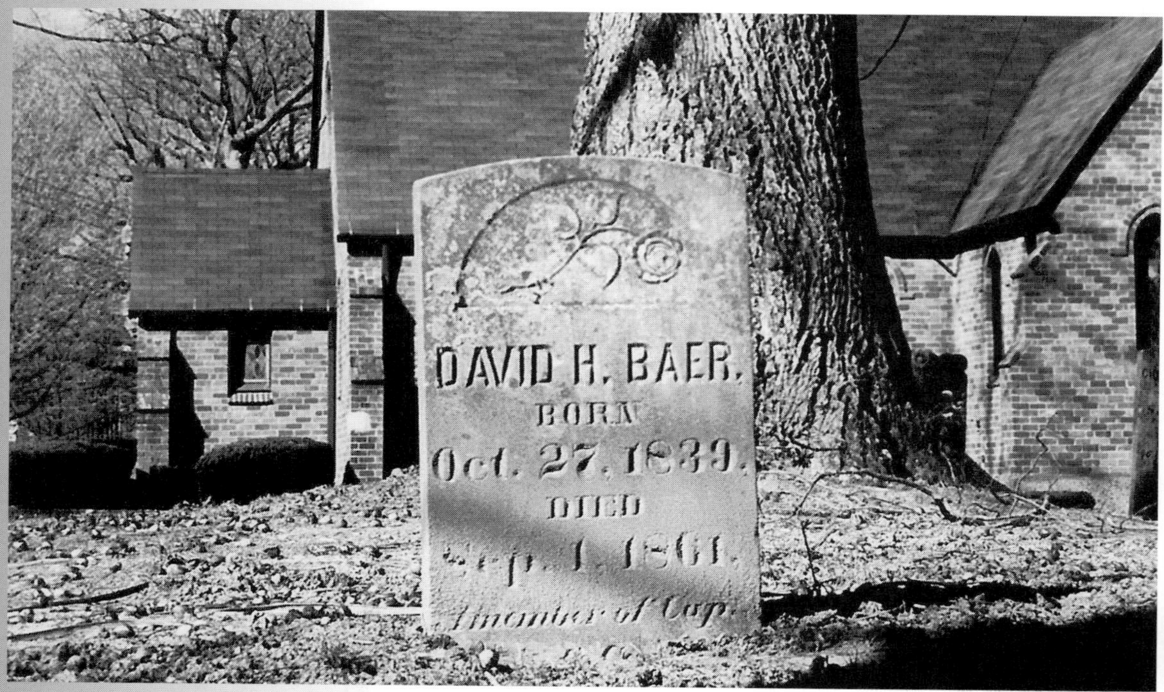

St. James Church Yard. David H. Baer was one of the first wartime deaths in the Churchville Cavalry, due to disease.

a former tailor. Additionally, Sterrett's fiancée, Miss Alanza Rounds, provided a blue cashmere dress that was used in the making of the company flag. While the men continued to assemble and wait for their uniforms, they drilled near Loch Willow Academy, where wives and sweethearts would gather to watch the assembly of horsemen.

On May 12, the company received orders to march to Staunton where they received yet another flag and a sendoff speech by former Secession Delegate George Baylor. Countermarching through Churchville on May 13, the company bivouacked for the evening at Buffalo Gap. Eventually the Churchville Cavalry reached Philippi in Barbour County and commenced regular service in the Confederate Army.

From the driveway of the St. James Church, return to Hotchkiss Road and turn right toward Rt. 250. Turn right on Rt. 250 East/Churchville Avenue and proceed .2 miles. The Hanger marker will be on the left.

James Edward Hanger Marker — Stop No. 18

While at Philippi, the Churchville Cavalry, as a part of Col. George A. Porterfield's force of approximately 750 men, was attacked before dawn on June 3, 1861. When the Federal artillery opened, the Confederates were taken by surprise and immediately began to evacuate. In addition to losing one of the company flags, the Churchville Cavalry also had two men wounded in the fray. James Edward Hanger was one of the casualties and later recalled:

> The first two shots were canister and directed at the Cavalry Camps, the third shot was a 6 pound solid shot aimed at the stable in which the Churchville Cavalry Company had slept. This shot struck the ground, ricocheted, entering the stable and struck me. I remained in the stable till they came looking for plunder, about four hours after I was wounded.

With no hope of saving Hanger's limb, Dr. James D. Robinson, of the 16th Ohio Infantry removed it, performing what is believed to have been the first amputation of the war. Exchanged as a prisoner of war at Norfolk in August 1861, Hanger returned to Churchville and remained in his room for weeks. After three months of whittling and working with barrel staves and scraps of wood, Hanger finally emerged from his room and walked down the stairs on an artificial leg that hinged at the knee.

James E. Hanger.
Courtesy of Hanger Orthopedic Group, Inc.

After he patented his invention, the Virginia Legislature contracted with him to make limbs for wounded veterans. Hanger thereby began his long career in prosthetics, with offices in Staunton and Richmond. The demand for artificial limbs continued to boom well after the war

Hanger historic marker.

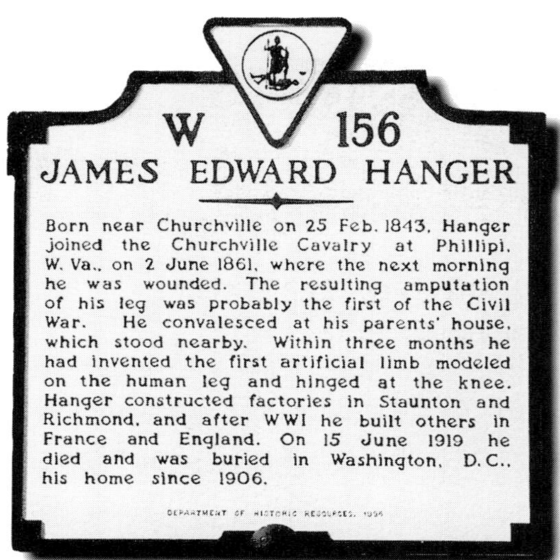

and, by the time he died in 1919, J. E. Hanger, Inc. had branches in London, Paris, Philadelphia, Pittsburgh, Atlanta, and St. Louis. The modern Hanger Orthopedic Company is still one of the fastest growing companies in the United States.

W 156
JAMES EDWARD HANGER
Born near Churchville on 25 Feb. 1843, Hanger joined the Churchville Cavalry at Phillipi, W. Va., on 2 June 1861, where the next morning he was wounded. The resulting amputation of his leg was probably the first of the Civil War. He convalesced at his parents' house, which stood nearby. Within three months he had invented the first artificial limb modeled on the human leg and hinged at the knee. Hanger constructed factories in Staunton and Richmond, and after WWI he built others in France and England. On 15 June 1919 he died and was buried in Washington, D.C., his home since 1906.

An article from a summer edition of the *Richmond Whig* summarized well the status of Augusta County in 1861:

> Augusta county . . . has had a heavy burden to bear, but she bears it out cheerfully. She has about 2,230 men in the military service. One half of her white agricultural labour is withdrawn from its ordinary pursuits. She has also been obliged to supply a large proportion of the animal labor used in the transportation of provisions and munitions to the western camps. Almost every farmer has been required to surrender one or more wagons and teams, and there is reason to fear that the withdrawal of so much labor, both human and animal, may seriously affect the next year's crop. But all are in good spirits and unalterably fixed in the determination to resist to the last Yankee aggression, and never again to be in political fellowship with those who have shown themselves willing to surrender the writ of habeas corpus, and every other safeguard of liberty, into the hands of an arbitrary despot.

TOUR NO. 2 April–May 1862, A Veil of Mystery and Deception: The Road to McDowell

Begin Tour No. 2 at the Rockfish Gap Tourist Information Center (Stop No. 19) near the Augusta/Nelson County border. Refer to the maps on pages 122–125 for assistance in locating the sites on this tour. This tour is approximately 76 miles in length and includes 8 stops at historic buildings and sites.

Gen. John C. Fremont.
Courtesy of
the National Archives

Just over a month after Gen. Thomas J. "Stonewall" Jackson's defeat at the Battle of Kernstown, near Winchester, the Confederate Valley Army spent nearly two weeks reorganizing at Conrad's Store (Elkton) in eastern Rockingham County. By the end of April, Jackson was determined to move on the offensive. With Gen. John C. Fremont's Federal army threatening Staunton from the west and Gen. Nathaniel Banks' army bearing down on Jackson from the Luray Valley and across the Massanutten Mountain at New Market, Jackson needed to move quickly and strike Fremont before he could unite with Banks. As a part of the plan, Jackson planned on uniting with Gen. Edward "Allegheny" Johnson's army at West View, just west of Staunton. Once the Confederate forces had combined, Jackson could attack and defeat Fremont, thereby giving Jackson the flexibility to deal with Banks' army. Meanwhile, to keep Banks' army at bay during this maneuvering, Confederate Gen. Richard S. Ewell moved his division across the Blue Ridge from near Stanardsville in Greene County toward Conrad's Store.

Rockfish Gap and the Virginia Central Railroad — Stop No. 19

Having left his encampment at Conrad's Store by 3 a.m. on April 30, Stonewall Jackson marched his army, in horrible conditions of rain and mud, toward Port Republic and Brown's Gap, where it crossed the Blue Ridge. One member of the Stonewall Brigade remembered Jackson "getting rocks, and putting them in the holes" in the road to aid in the passage of the wagons. By May 3, as the weather began to clear, Jackson's army moved down along the eastern face of the mountains to Mechum's River Station on the Virginia Central

AMERICAN HOTEL

Edward Byer's drawing of Staunton, Virginia, from Sears Hill.
Geography and Map Division, Library of Congress

Right: Gen. Thomas J. "Stonewall" Jackson.
Courtesy of the National Archives

Far right: Gen. Turner Ashby.
From *Stonewall Jackson's Way*

From the Rockfish Gap Tourists Information Center, take Rt. 250 West for 3.6 miles and merge right remaining on Rt. 250/Broad Street in Waynesboro. Continue on Rt. 250 West for approximately 11 miles to Staunton. The Staunton Depot is on S. Augusta Street.

Railroad. On the following day, trains began taking most of Jackson's army back across the Blue Ridge while Jackson, along with his more able-bodied men, wagons, and guns, made the march across Rockfish Gap. One member of the Rockbridge Artillery later recalled, "To our astonishment we recrossed the mountain, from the top of which we again gazed on that grand old Valley, and felt that our homes might still be ours." That same day, early before dawn, word had come from Gen. "Allegheny" Johnson of General Fremont's advance toward Staunton.

Stop No. 7b

Staunton Depot

Having heard of Jackson's departure from the Valley, and with news of Fremont's advance toward Staunton, the streets of town were full of depressing rumors of impending disaster. Nevertheless, locals went about their daily lives and filled the churches of the town in hopeful prayer. By 11 a.m. on Sunday, May 4, it would appear that many a prayer had been answered as train whistles gave the first indication that something was afoot. Locals crowded the depot and gave the ragged soldiers of Jackson's army a warm welcome as they offloaded from the cars. Arriving by horseback later that day, Jackson became alarmed at the public enthusiasm, fearing that word would reach the enemy of the army's return to the Valley. Jackson immediately tasked Col. Turner Ashby's cavalry with sealing off the town, allowing no one in or out to spread the news of his army's arrival.

From the Staunton Depot, proceed to S. Lewis Street and turn right. Proceed for approximately .1 miles and turn right on W. Johnson Street. The site of the Virginia Hotel is on the corner of Johnson/Greenville Avenue and New Street. It is now a parking garage.

SITE OF THE VIRGINIA HOTEL — STOP NO. 20A

After Jackson had established his headquarters at the Virginia Hotel, he began to receive word that his ruse was working. By Monday, May 5, Jackson had learned that the Federals were placing his army at any number of locations across the map from Richmond to Gordonsville to Staunton and even back to Harrisonburg. General Banks, meanwhile, deeming Harrisonburg as unimportant and overly exposed, withdrew his forces to New Market.

That same day, some two hundred cadets of the Virginia Military Institute arrived. After being put up in a long barracks where the National Valley Bank building now stands, on May 6, the Corps gave the general a dress parade. To make himself more presentable for the occasion, Jackson had a haircut and exchanged his blue U.S. major's uniform that he had worn at VMI for a gray one with the insignia of a Confederate general. At the Virginia Hotel that day, ladies of the town began pacing about the outside of it, awaiting a glimpse of the famous hero of Manassas. "When he saw our eager faces," noted one, "he took off his hat, smiled and passed on." Before 6:30 a.m. on May 7, Jackson's command finally set off to unite with General Johnson, with Gen. William B. Taliaferro's brigade leading the way out of town. To continue the deception, Jackson, without notice to his staff, mounted his horse and headed south along the Middlebrook Road away from the path of his army. His staff hurried to catch up with the general, but he finally took a right onto a byroad that brought him back along the Staunton and Parkersburg Turnpike to the balance of his marching troops.

From the corner of Johnson and New Streets, continue north to Frederick Street and turn left. Continue on Frederick Street for approximately .7 miles and turn right on W. Beverley Street. This road becomes Parkersburg Turnpike after leaving Staunton city limits. From the corner of Frederick and Beverley, proceed for approximately 5.6 miles to West View. There is a turn off and a Virginia Civil War Trails marker at the United Methodist Church on the right.

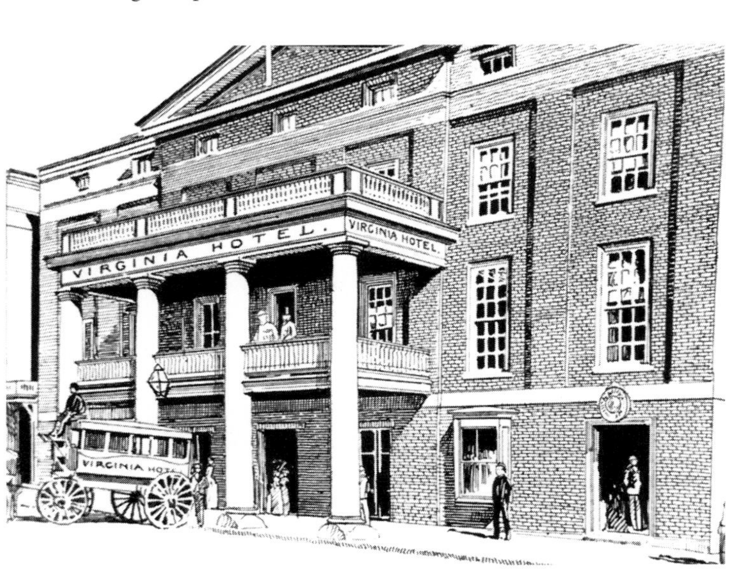

Late nineteenth-century view of Virginia Hotel.
FROM THE HAMRICK COLLECTION

Stop No. 21 West View

Gen. Edward "Allegheny" Johnson.
Courtesy of the United States Army Military History Institute

After evacuating Shenandoah Mountain on April 18, Confederate forces under General Johnson moved into camp here, around the village of West View. As his Confederates made their way through Buffalo Gap on April 20, Federal troops engaged Johnson's rear guard briefly before pulling back. Over 3,600 men in two brigades settled into their temporary home in the fields east and west of the village. General Johnson made his headquarters at nearby Valley Mills in the home of Capt. Philip O. Palmer. Jedediah Hotchkiss, under orders from General Jackson, visited Johnson at the Palmer home on April 27 and 28 to discuss the enemy's position in Ramsey's Draft on Shenandoah Mountain.

Lt. Septimus Williams of the 58th Virginia Infantry described the new site: "We are here in the renowned Valley of Virginia. It is a lovely spot on the green earth. Some beautiful residences, fine lands, wheat and the different grasses are looking delightful, but I tell you that an army will spread destruction in its course. Splendid fields of wheat are thrown out to the commons and are being trodden under feet of man and beast, not even sparing fences around gardens. Some take kindly, while others show evident signs of displeasure." While in camp at West View, Johnson's army reorganized and, by May 2, conducted a review.

While you stand at the West View Civil War Trails marker, the paved road that you see is actually on the original grade of the Parkersburg Turnpike.

By Monday, May 5, word of Jackson's arrival in Staunton had reached Johnson's men. Charles C. Wright, adjutant of the 58th Virginia Infantry, wrote that ". . . our camp is aroused and excited . . . by the report that Gen. Jackson is marching . . . to join us. . . . In the midst of our wondering and planning comes an order for us to prepare to move and to have three days rations in our haversacks. . . . By the end of the day some of Jackson's troops marched up and camped nearby."

Philip O. Palmer House at Valley Mills. (Site A)

This bridge abutment on the east bank of the Middle River at Valley Mills reveals a part of the original path of the old Parkersburg Turnpike where Johnson's and Jackson's men crossed in 1862.

The Parkersburg Turnpike

Stop No. 22

The Parkersburg to Staunton Turnpike, initially authorized in 1826, was planned and laid out by Claudius Crozet, the state engineer of Virginia. It was not built until the 1840s, however, with completion of the main roadway in 1848. When completed, the turnpike was recognized as an engineering marvel. The road crossed high mountains and led deep into western Virginia. By the time of the war, however, the road had fallen into disrepair at several points and was becoming difficult to traverse.

Jackson's Foot Cavalry.
From *Battles and Leaders of the Civil War*

One of the abutments of the early turnpike bridges can be found approximately .7 miles to the west on the Middle River. Likewise, the Palmer home, where Johnson headquartered in April and May 1862, can be seen near the bridge abutment. However, because there is no adequate safe pull-off near either site, both sites can be difficult to see. Therefore, from the stop at West View, proceed west on Rt. 254 for 4.3 miles and stop at the Buffalo Gap Presbyterian Church. This is the original route of the old Parkersburg Turnpike. Because it is a difficult road to traverse, especially in foul weather, the tour will be redirected to Rt. 42 and will regain the old turnpike at a later point. From the Buffalo Gap Presbyterian Church, head east on Rt. 254 for .8 miles and turn left onto Rt. 42. Proceed for 5.2 miles to Churchville. Turn left on Churchville Avenue/Rt. 250 West. Proceed for approximately 15 miles (you will regain the old Parkersburg Turnpike along the way near the village of West Augusta) to the next stop at Mountain House where you will also find another Virginia Civil War Trails marker.

Stop No. 23 — Site of Mountain House

Gen. Robert H. Milroy.
From *Generals in Blue*/Warner Collection

By noon on Tuesday, May 6, Johnson had his army on the road again, marching west from West View toward North Mountain. The Valley Army, meanwhile, started from Staunton on May 7, following Johnson's army.

With the 52nd Virginia in the lead and Lt. "Bent" Coiner commanding the advance guard, Federals of the 1st West Virginia Cavalry were driven from the junction of the Harrisonburg-Warm Springs and Staunton-Parkersburg Turnpikes, over Shenandoah Mountain. The 31st Virginia was then ordered to the front to reinforce the 52nd, but they arrived only in time to see a few dead horses and riders. Farther on, here, near Rodgers' Toll House, portions of Gen. Robert Milroy's Federal Brigade (3rd West Virginia, 32nd Ohio, and 75th Ohio Infantries) were stunned as a cavalryman rode through the camp yelling "the rebels are coming!" After a brief clash, the Federals hastily withdrew, abandoning their baggage before retreating to the crest of Shenandoah Mountain.

Jim Hall of the 31st Virginia Infantry wrote that they had started early on the morning of May 7 and "marched to the western side of Shenandoah Mountain. The enemy held the top of the Mountain, but fled without any resistance. A considerable picket fight occurred as we approached the mountain. The enemy lost two men killed, two prisoners and three horses. We lost none. As we approached the ravines on the western side of the mountain, the enemy opened on us with a 12-pounder rifle cannon [at Shaw's Fork]. They did no execution more than to arrest our advance until morning."

From the Mountain House stop, continue west on Rt. 250 for 2.1 miles to Fort Edward Johnson at the top of Shenandoah Mountain on the Augusta/Highland County line. Fort Johnson is now within National Forest boundaries. There is a .5 mile self-guided walking tour that allows excellent views of the earthworks and breathtaking views of the surrounding area. Interpretive signage along the way also gives excellent insight into the Confederate experience here.

Though no longer standing, Mountain House was a major stop along the Parkersburg Turnpike on the way to McDowell and Monterey.

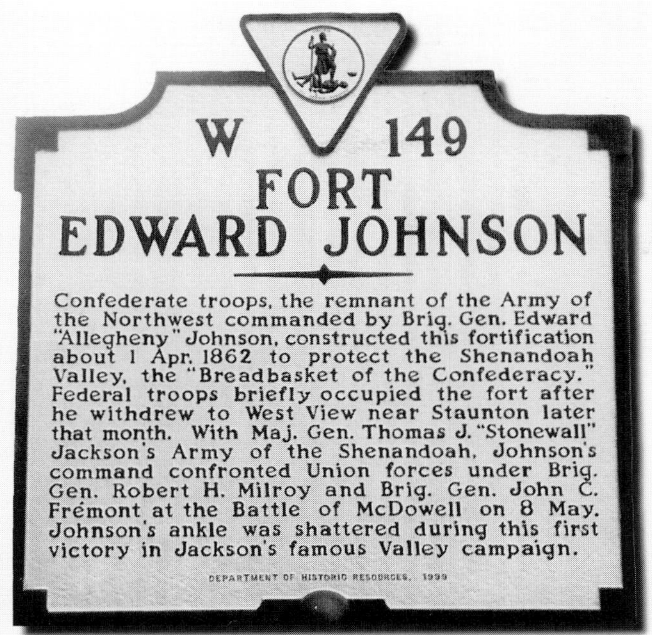

Historic marker at Fort Edward Johnson.

Fort Edward Johnson — Stop No. 24

Johnson's army, followed by Jackson's Valley Army, passed this point unopposed on its march to McDowell. Initially, the advancing Confederates were concerned that the Federals might take advantage of the works here, developed only a month before by Johnson's men. However, these concerns were dispelled through a reconnaissance of the position.

Under orders of Gen. Robert E. Lee, Johnson's troops had abandoned their position at Allegheny Mountain on April 1, following Jackson's defeat at Kernstown. Marching to Shenandoah Mountain, another strong position was constructed and later dubbed "Fort Edward Johnson," in honor of the commanding general. One officer in Johnson's command wrote: "We are nearly on top of the great Shenandoah Mountain which is very strong, will be impregnable in a few days. They have done an immense amount of work since they have been here, such as cutting timber, ditching, fortifying in different ways. We have some mud here as well as elsewhere, notwithstanding we are on the mountains." After having been forced to leave this site in mid-April, one of the men wrote: "I am sorry we had to leave Camp Shenandoah, Oh, it was a magnificent place, good water, good camping, the healthiest place we have been, as yet. Our mail facilities were just as good as we could wish, nearly, we had daily mail. We were well fortified, having 12 pieces of cannon, well arranged. . . ."

The earthworks are plainly visible throughout the walking tour at Fort Johnson. This rebuilt section shows how the works were fortified with logs.

On May 8, 1862, Jackson descended on McDowell in Highland County and was attacked by Milroy's and Brig. Gen. Robert C. Schenck's brigades. As senior officer on the field, Schenck held command of the Federal troops for the battle. Fighting commenced at 10 a.m. and continued on until dark, when the Federal troops withdrew from the battlefield. Early on May 9, Schenck ordered a general retreat to Franklin. For nearly a week, Jackson pursued the Federals almost to Franklin before commencing a return march to the Valley on May 15.

Though not a part of this self-guided tour of Augusta County sites, from Fort Edward Johnson, you can continue on to the McDowell Battlefield. The first interpretive markers can be found approximately 7.4 miles on the right. This stop also offers a 1.5-mile walking tour that will take you to the top of Sitlington Hill. For a continued driving experience that will take you into the lines of the Union soldiers, continue on for approximately 1.8 miles for more Virginia Civil War Trails interpretive markers.

From Fort Edward Johnson, continue approximately 16.7 miles back to Churchville. Turn left on Rt. 42 and, after 8.1 miles, turn left on Rt. 607/Moscow Loop (becomes Rt. 731/Natural Chimney Road). Proceed for 2.6 miles to the creek in the heart of the village of Mt. Solon.

Gen. Robert C. Schenck, commander of the Federal forces at the Battle of McDowell.
From *Generals in Blue*/
Warner Collection

STOP NO. 25: *Mt. Solon, looking eastward near the site of the mill where Jackson and Ewell met in May 1862.*

Early twentieth-century view of Mt. Solon.
FROM THE HAMRICK COLLECTION

STOP NO. 25

MT. SOLON

Gen. Richard S. Ewell.
FROM *PHOTOGRAPHIC HISTORY OF THE CIVIL WAR*

Upon his return from Franklin, Jackson sent a message to Ewell asking him to meet him for a conference. Early on the morning of Sunday, May 18, Ewell arrived at Jackson's headquarters near this site. While many of the men went into camp religious services at nearby Mossy Creek, the two generals went into conference at an old gristmill along this creek. Following discussion of the plans for the upcoming fight, Ewell ordered his division from Conrad's Store into the Page Valley. Jackson's men, in the meantime, moved toward Bridgewater the following morning. By May 21, Jackson's army was bearing down on General Banks' Federal Army at Strasburg. While Jackson was approaching along the Valley Turnpike, Ewell was moving down the Page Valley. Jackson in the midst of yet another ruse, turned his army west across the Massanutten, joined Ewell's command near Luray, and by May 23 was attacking the small Federal garrison at Front Royal. The attack caught Banks unexpectedly and forced his retreat to Winchester on May 24. The following day, Jackson struck again and was victorious. Within two weeks, Jackson had taken the threat away from Staunton and placed it not far from Washington, D.C.

TOUR NO. 3 JUNE 1862, AUGUSTA COUNTY DURING THE BATTLES OF HARRISONBURG, CROSS KEYS, AND PORT REPUBLIC

BEGIN TOUR NO. 3 AT THE SITE OF THE Academy (Stop No. 26) at the southwest corner of Wayne and Broad Streets in Waynesboro. Refer to the maps on pages 122–125 for assistance in locating the sites on this tour. This tour is approximately 29 miles in length and includes 4 stops at historic buildings and sites.

Gen. James Shields.
COURTESY OF THE NATIONAL ARCHIVES

In the wake of the Confederate victory at the Battle of Winchester, Jackson was once again threatened by a number of Federal armies. Though he had successfully driven General Banks' army from the Shenandoah Valley, the armies of Gen. John C. Fremont and Gen. James Shields threatened from Winchester along the Valley Pike and from Front Royal along the eastern side of Massanutten Mountain. If the two armies could unite, perhaps at New Market, the combined force would be numerically superior to Jackson's. However, the swiftness of Jackson's command and a river swollen by heavy rains stood in the way of the Federals. Unable to cross the South Fork of the Shenandoah River in Page County, Shields would have to continue to move toward Conrad's Store and Port Republic, while Fremont pressed south toward Harrisonburg. At the apex of the campaign, Jackson summarily defeated both armies in two days: Fremont on June 8 at the Battle of Cross Keys and Shields on June 9 at the Battle of Port Republic.

Following the Battles of Cross Keys and Port Republic, wounded streamed into Augusta County and field hospitals were set up at several sites along the county line east from Weyers Cave. Many casualties were eventually brought to the Confederate General Hospital at Staunton.

SITE OF THE ACADEMY — STOP NO. 26

While a number of casualties resulted from the two battles of June 8 and 9, one of the most significant losses of the 1862 Shenandoah Valley Campaign was the death of Gen. Turner Ashby on June 6 at the Battle of Harrisonburg. Having met the vanguard of General

The Academy.
FROM *WAYNESBORO DAYS OF YORE*

Fremont's forces, Ashby, leading two infantry regiments, was struck down late in the fight.

The following day, Ashby's body was taken to the Frank Kemper house in Port Republic, where it lay in state long enough for a brief funeral service and a chance for Jackson to gaze upon his fallen knight. The following morning, Ashby's body was taken to the village chapel where it remained until midday, after which the body was then escorted by a cortege up the east side of the South River to Waynesboro. Once there, the remains were placed briefly at the Academy and then removed across the street to the Chapman house. Later, the funeral cortege continued across the mountains to Charlottesville. On June 8, the famous cavalier was laid to rest in the University of Virginia Cemetery. In October 1866, Ashby's body was removed to Winchester for reburial in the Stonewall Cemetery alongside his brother Richard.

Gen. Turner Ashby's remains posed at the Kemper House in Port Republic.
PRIVATE COLLECTION

From the corner of Wayne and Broad, turn left on Broad and proceed .1 miles and turn right into Willow Oak Plaza where Rose Hall once stood.

Site of the Hugh Gallaher House/"Rose Hall," circa 1830

Stop No. 27a

As the Battle of Cross Keys raged, "Rose Hall" served as a gathering point for Federal prisoners of war. Local Dewitt C. Gallaher, a resident of Waynesboro and a soldier in the 1st Virginia Cavalry, recalled that the prisoners captured during the fight at Cross Keys and Port Republic were brought to Waynesboro and "put in the fields above our house."

John H. Worsham in 1864.
From *One of Jackson's Foot Cavalry*

Pvt. John Worsham remembered that, while guarding the prisoners at Waynesboro, the cannonading could be heard from the battle, and that, as "the prisoners were very excited, it would have taken very little to stampede them; every man was on duty, and it was a great strain on our men; and when more prisoners were brought to us, with the information that Jackson had defeated Fremont, the relief was almost overpowering. Amongst a small squad of prisoners, brought us here by some cavalry, was an Englishman, captured on the 6th, calling himself Sir Percy Wyndham. He was a colonel in the Yankee army, and, it is said, requested to be sent to the Valley, as he would capture the rebel Ashby the first time he got within striking distance of him. Ashby with some of his cavalry met Sir Percy near Harrisonburg and among the first men taken by Ashby's men was this same Sir Percy." Ironically, only the day before, Ashby's body had lain in state not far from where the boastful Wyndham stood now as a prisoner of war.

Worsham continued, "He [Wyndham] was made to march on foot with other prisoners from the place of capture to Waynesboro, and

The Hugh Gallaher House/"Rose Hall."
From *Waynesboro Days of Yore*

Col. Sir Percy Wyndham.
COURTESY OF THE UNITED STATES ARMY MILITARY HISTORY INSTITUTE

From the "Rose Hall" site at Willow Oak Plaza, turn left on Broad Street and proceed for .7 miles and turn left on Main Street. Proceed .15 miles and turn left onto Rt. 340 North. Proceed for 14.4 miles to the town of Grottoes in Rockingham County. Turn left onto Third Street/Rt. 256 and travel for 2.2 miles and turn left on Battlefield Road/Rt. 608. The Stonewall Jackson Prayer Oak is just to the left along the old road grade in the field. The house where he took his breakfast is to the right of the road.

when he reached us, was the most exasperated man I had seen for a long time. He said that in his army (the English), when an officer of his rank was captured, he was taken charge of by an officer of like rank, and treated accordingly, until exchanged or paroled. Here he was marched through mud and mire, and that too, by a rebel private; it was enough to make a saint swear." The Federal prisoners were marched across Rockfish Gap later that evening.

STOP NO. 28

STONEWALL JACKSON PRAYER OAK

By June 12, following the Battle of Port Republic, Jackson had established new headquarters. Hotchkiss described the new site as "in the corner of the woods where the Weyers Cave Road leaves the Port Republic Road." Meanwhile, the Army of the Valley made camp in the fields between Weyers Cave and Mt. Meridian.

A former minister of Augusta County's Tinkling Spring Presbyterian Church (1847) and Jackson's chief of staff, Rev. Robert Louis Dabney, wrote that the location was a "smiling paradise in a range of woodland groves . . . surrounded with the verdure of early summer and the luxuriant wheatfields whitening to the harvest."

As troops went into camp, Hotchkiss recalled that Jackson ordered "washing and cleaning up to be done." Many men also took the opportunity for rest and relaxation by visiting the famous local cave.

On Saturday, June 14, Jackson ordered that the day be recognized as one of thanksgiving and he ordered general courts-martial to convene as necessary. On what Hotchkiss described as "a very warm day," the men assembled for religious services by 3 p.m. When services concluded at sundown, preaching commenced and was carried on

Rev. Robert L. Dabney.
FROM *DISCUSSIONS*

Stonewall Jackson's Prayer Oak.

Though not drawn to show a particular location, this sketch gives a fine example of one of Jackson's many camp prayer meetings.
FROM *FOUR YEARS IN THE STONEWALL BRIGADE*

Return to Rt. 256 West/Weyers Cave Road and proceed 4.65 miles and turn left on Rt. 11 South. Proceed approximately 6.75 miles into Staunton to S. Augusta Street and turn left to reach the Staunton Depot. Note that at 4.3 miles you can see Augusta Military Academy, which was started after the war by Confederate veteran Charles Summerville Roller. Roller, a former member of the "Valley Rangers" of Company E, 1st Virginia Cavalry and colonel of the 160th Virginia Militia, also served, after the war, as a member of the Virginia House of Delegates, principal of the Virginia School for the Deaf and Blind, and was a member of the Stonewall Jackson Camp of Confederate Veterans. At 4.6 miles you can stop at Willow Spout and the site of Hanger's Tavern which was frequented by many travelers on the old Valley Pike during the war.

well into the evening. The next morning—being a Sunday—divine services were held with Rev. Robert L. Dabney delivering the message in the morning. That evening, the holy sacrament was administered. Private Joseph F. Kauffman of the 10th Virginia Infantry noted that "Gen. Jackson partook with the multitude."

According to local tradition, Jackson, while camped close by, took breakfast on the front porch of the nearby house every morning. To give the general privacy during his meal, it is said the family of the house hung blankets around the porch. Following breakfast, Jackson stopped under this tree to pray.

Right: Charles Summerville Roller. (Site B)
COURTESY OF AUGUSTA MILITARY ACADEMY

Opposite Page: Hanger's Tavern. (Site C)
FROM THE HAMRICK COLLECTION

Stop No. 7c — Staunton Depot

Gen. William Henry Chase Whiting.
From *Generals in Gray*/
Warner Collection

Wishing to reinforce Jackson for another offensive, Gen. Robert E. Lee dispatched reinforcements to the Valley. Gen. Chase Whiting's Division of two brigades as well as Gen. Alexander Lawton's Georgia Brigade and a North Carolina Battalion arrived at the Staunton Depot on June 16. With the new troops, Jackson's numbers swelled to approximately 8,000 men. By the following day, under instruction from Jackson, rumors were circulated down the Valley that he was beginning to move forward on another offensive with 20,000 men. However, in truth, he ordered Whiting's men to retrain at Staunton for travel to Gordonsville, and he prepared the balance of his army for a march to Charlottesville. Late that evening, Jackson arrived in Staunton, along with his cousin, William L. Jackson, and took quarters for the night. The following morning, Jackson left Staunton for the last time when he boarded a train in order to join his men at Waynesboro. By June 19, the men began arriving at Mechum's Depot and boarded trains bound for Richmond. Following his victorious Shenandoah Valley Campaign, Jackson was on his way to reinforce General Lee in the defense of Richmond. Throughout that summer, the Army of Northern Virginia would see victories from the Seven Days Battles to Cedar Mountain, Second Manassas, and Chantilly, before turning west into the Shenandoah Valley on a march that would lead to the first invasion of the North and the subsequent Battle of Sharpsburg.

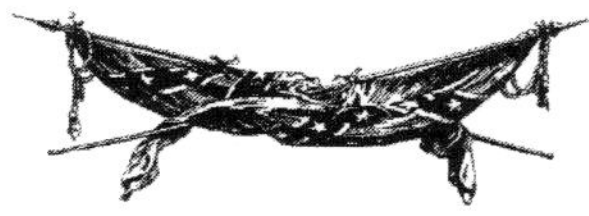

TOUR NO. 4 1863, A HOSPITAL TOWN AND RAILHEAD FOR PRISONERS OF WAR

Circa 1880 view of Staunton from near Frederick Street. This area was occupied by many of the shops of the Confederate military depot.
FROM THE HAMRICK COLLECTION

BEGIN TOUR NO. 4 AT THE SITE OF THE Virginia School for the Deaf and Blind (Stop No. 8B) on E. Beverley Street in Staunton. Refer to the maps on pages 122–125 for assistance in locating the sites on this tour. This tour is approximately 2 miles in length and includes 3 stops at historic buildings and sites.

By 1863, Staunton was well into its second year of serving as a major railhead for the Confederacy. A town teaming with vital industries, including grist and saw mills, and factories that produced wagons, shoes, boots, woolen clothing, and blankets, Staunton had a great deal to offer the Confederacy. In less than two years, thousands of troops from throughout the South had traveled by train through the Staunton Depot en route to various points in western and eastern Virginia. Also, the railhead served as a marketing opportunity for farmers of the "Breadbasket of the Confederacy" and for the many supplies being turned out by the local supply depot, quartermaster, and commissary post.

However, during 1863, a year of both crucial high and low points in the life of the Confederacy, Staunton would remain relatively quiet in comparison to the year before and the year that would follow, with one exception. In the wake of the great battles that were to be fought that year, Staunton, with a major Confederate Army Hospital, would serve as host to nearly 8,500 wounded and sick Confederate and Union soldiers.

Stop No. 8b

Virginia School for the Deaf and Blind

Though these buildings had served as the Institute for the Deaf, Dumb and Blind before the war, in 1861, the residents were redirected to the Virginia Female Institute (the future Stuart Hall) and this site was converted into a Confederate Military Hospital.

By August 1861, it was reported that the hospital was already host to "500 sick soldiers." While major combat had not reached the area, the majority of the men suffered from a broad range of diseases including pneumonia, measles, mumps, typhoid fever, and dysentery. With few

Early view of the Virginia School for the Deaf and Blind.
From the Hamrick Collection

Gen. William Dorsey Pender.
FROM *LEE'S LIEUTENANTS*

men available to serve as nurses, ladies of the town came out in numbers to "minister tenderly" to the patients' needs "as far as possible."

After the Battle of Gettysburg, the hospital saw a great influx of wounded as the Army of Northern Virginia used the Shenandoah Valley as a retreat route back into the Old Dominion. Among those brought to Staunton was Gen. William D. Pender who, on July 18, breathed his last, saying quietly, "Tell my wife that I do not fear to die. I can confidently resign my soul to God, trusting in the atonement of Jesus Christ. My only regret is to leave her and our two children. I have always tried to do my duty in every sphere in which Providence has placed me."

The many men brought here filled the wards of the hospital frequently forcing reliance on local private residences where the wounded could recover or die. One local, Col. William D. Stuart of the 56th Virginia Infantry, wounded in Pickett's Charge on July 3, 1863, was brought back to the vacated Virginia Female Institute where he, along with others after Gettysburg, was a patient. Stuart died on July 30.

From the entrance of the VSDB campus on Beverley Street, head west toward N. Coalter Street and turn right. Proceed .15 miles and turn left on E. Frederick. Continue for .8 miles and turn right on W. Beverley Street. The entrance to Thornrose Cemetery is .1 miles on the right. After passing under the entrance arch, continue straight for .1 miles under the stone bridge, turn right and continue .05 miles before turning left and continuing yet another .05 miles. The Confederate section will be on your right.

THORNROSE CEMETERY — STOP NO. 29

Since Staunton was the site of a significant Confederate hospital, it was natural that the town would also have to find room for the many dead that would not be claimed during the war. With the coming of the Civil War, Thornrose Cemetery became that site.

Established in 1849, Thornrose Cemetery's first interment was a slave, buried here in 1853. Two months later the cemetery was officially dedicated on May 28, 1853.

ANDERSON P FLOWERS
MUS CO A 38 GA INF
WRIGHTS LEGION
CONFEDERATE STATES ARMY
JAN 21 1845 JAN 20 1863

One of the modern grave markers in the Confederate section of Thornrose Cemetery. Regrettably, while the names of most of the soldiers buried are known, there is no surviving record as to where each man now lies.

By the spring of 1861, Thornrose had been operating as a cemetery for less than eight years. Though not a patient of the hospital, Thornrose's first Confederate interment came on July 9, 1861. Pvt. D. C. McLeweray of the 3rd Arkansas Infantry was accidentally killed by one of the cars at the depot when his regiment was detraining. Eleven days later, Halifax County native, Pvt. Alexander J. Wall of Company K, 20th Virginia Infantry, was the next to be buried, and the first son of Old Virginia's Confederates to be laid to rest here.

Though many more Confederates were buried in the coming months, not until March 1862 was there a system for the burials. In addition to those buried here during the war, after the war had ended, a project was initiated in which the bodies of Confederate dead could be gathered and reburied here from many of the surrounding battlefields. Though an effort was made into the early twentieth century to maintain the identification of the graves, today, the graves of approximately 1,800 Confederates buried here are unmarked. The majority of the modern markers now in place were installed in more recent years without knowledge of the actual burial sites of the few named soldiers.

From Thornrose Cemetery, turn left on W. Beverley Street and proceed for .7 miles. Turn right on Augusta Street and continue .05 miles to the Staunton Depot.

STAUNTON DEPOT: RAILHEAD TO PRISONERS OF WAR CAMPS

STOP NO. 7D

While Staunton's Confederate Military Hospital played host to many Confederates, it also served several Union soldiers left on the field of battle or in private residences near where they were captured. If they recovered and were not paroled or exchanged, their next stop was generally here at the Staunton Depot where, like many of those who had been captured but not necessarily wounded, they boarded trains bound for prisoner of war camps throughout the South.

Two excellent accounts of Federal officers arriving in Staunton as Prisoners of War are available in the memoirs of Captain (later Colonel) Samuel M. Quincy of the 2nd Massachusetts Infantry and Lt. Col. Frederick F. Cavada of the 114th Pennsylvania Infantry (Collis' Zouaves).

Quincy was wounded and captured at Cedar Mountain in August 1862. According to his recollections, after arriving by rail, "the Yankees were looked upon like animals in a menagerie by the curious inhabitants." Since the Confederate wounded were taken off first, Quincy was not carried off the train until later that evening. As he rode through town toward the hospital, he recalled the women standing in the windows with "various expressions of countenance, pity being the scarcest."

Captured at Gettysburg, Cavada recalled his entry into Staunton on July 18. "We were a squalid set, way-worn and weary, and covered with the dust of long foot-travel; with haggard faces, and uncombed hair; some carrying their wounded arms in slings; many with bare and lacerated feet; and all bearing the unmistakable impress of the days of hunger, exposure, and fatigue, through which we had just passed . . . for near three weeks we had lived chiefly on flour-paste and water." Cavada commented that the Shenandoah Valley "was a beautiful country . . . but it had presented no charms to weary eyes that were compelled to view it through a line of hostile bayonets."

Following the influx of casualties from the Battle of Gettysburg, Staunton again fell relatively quiet, though casualties and sick from the army did continue to arrive. In November 1863, the local Augusta Raid Guard was called out to Shenandoah Mountain to repel Federal troops rumored to be advancing on Staunton. Most of the companies of the Guard had just been formed during the summer and served under the command of veterans John Baldwin and Kenton Harper. Ultimately the alarm proved false and the men returned to Staunton.

View from West View toward Buffalo Gap.

On December 11, the Raid Guard was again called out and this time the threat was real. Gen. John D. Imboden's cavalry had already engaged the enemy force. Though not engaged, the Guard fell-in where they could. Additional troops from Gen. Jubal Early's command arrived in Staunton on December 15 and were hurried to Buffalo Gap. Leaving the regulars to deal with the enemy, the men of the Guard returned to their homes. Once again, however, at 10 p.m. on December 19, the signal cannon was fired and the Guard assembled. Following a day behind Early's infantry, the Confederates force-marched toward Harrisonburg. But by the time they arrived the enemy had retreated again. While the infantry continued on to Woodstock, the Augusta Raid Guard returned home. The Guard disbanded in early 1864, but many of the men were probably reorganized into reserve organizations that would be greatly needed in the defense of the county during the following spring.

TOUR NO. 5 May 1864, The Road to New Market

Begin Tour No. 5 at the site of the Staunton Depot (Stop No. 7E) in Staunton. Refer to the maps on pages 122–125 for assistance in locating the sites on this tour. This tour is approximately 4.4 miles in length and includes 3 stops at historic buildings and sites.

Staunton Depot — Stop No. 7E

Gen. Franz Sigel.
Courtesy of the National Archives

As Gen. Ulysses S. Grant opened his campaign in the spring of 1864, he ordered Maj. Gen. Franz Sigel to move up the Shenandoah Valley toward Staunton to destroy the Virginia Central Railroad line there. Then, Sigel was to move to Lynchburg on the east side of the Blue Ridge and destroy the rail line there as well. On May 10, 1864, Confederate Maj. Gen. John C. Breckinridge, the former senator and vice president of the United States, arrived in Staunton to organize resistance to Sigel's advance.

In Staunton, Breckinridge was also close to his familial roots as his father had been born at nearby "Glenmore." In the current crisis, however, there was no time for sentimental visits. Breckinridge spared no time in sending couriers up and down the Shenandoah Valley, preparing for the defense against Sigel's advancing army. One courier had been sent to the Virginia Military Institute in Lexington with a dispatch summoning the cadets to reinforce Breckinridge.

By May 11, Staunton was alive with activity as Breckinridge assembled his army and prepared to move down the Valley. That day, a portion of Gen. Gabriel Wharton's Brigade arrived at the railroad depot aboard the steam engine "Millboro." After detraining, the infantry marched two miles north of town on the Valley Pike and went into camp to await the arrival of the rest of the brigade, which was marching from Dublin Depot. A few of the men took advantage of the close proximity of the supply depot, and they were issued new jackets, socks, hats, shirts, and knapsacks.

In addition to the influx of soldiers from outside the county, Col. William H. Harman, acting under orders of General Breckinridge, called together the Augusta Reserves, an assemblage of 500 to 1,000 men from all points across the county.

From the Staunton Depot, proceed .1 miles to Lewis Street and turn right. Proceed for another .1 miles and turn right onto W. Johnson Street/Rt. 11. Proceed for 2.2 miles to Mountain View Drive on the left.

Gen. John C. Breckinridge.
COURTESY OF THE LIBRARY OF CONGRESS

STOP NO. 30 WHARTON'S BIVOUAC

On May 12, Breckinridge allowed the men a day of rest in camp as he made final plans to march in search of Sigel. The cadets from Lexington arrived the same day and filed into camp near the veterans of Gen. Gabriel C. Wharton's Brigade. One cadet later noted that the veterans made fun of the youths. "A tall, round-shouldered fellow, whose legs seemed almost split up to his shoulder blades, came among us with a pair of shears and a pack of playing cards, offering to take our names and cut off love-locks to be sent home after we were dead; another inquired if we wanted rosewood coffins, satin-lined, with name and age on the plate."

A handful of the young men slipped into town, despite having been restricted to camp for the evening. Cadet Carrington Taylor took four other cadets to his home to enjoy a good home-cooked dinner. Before

Gen. Gabriel C. Wharton.
COURTESY OF THE LIBRARY OF CONGRESS

departing, Mrs. Taylor asked the four boys to watch after her son. Ironically, of the party of five, Taylor would be the only one to avoid injury in the upcoming battle. At least five other cadets in the corps at the time also hailed from Staunton, including William B. Crawford, Carter H. Harrison (whose home was at nearby "West Hill"), John Andrew Stuart, Alexander H. H. Stuart Jr., and Charles W. Turner.

From this point you can break off from the Augusta County tour and continue north along the Valley Pike, covering the same ground marched by Breckinridge's army in May 1864, to New Market and the excellent State Battlefield Park there. Otherwise, you may return south along Rt. 11 to Staunton. The distance to the Staunton Depot is just over 2 miles.

At sunrise on May 13, Breckinridge's army began to make its way from Staunton along the Valley Pike. It passed by Cline's Mill and through Mt. Sidney and Burketown before entering Rockingham County. Two days later, Breckinridge's army made contact with Sigel's Federals on the outskirts of New Market. The subsequent battle resulted in the last Confederate victory in the Shenandoah Valley.

Staunton Depot — Stop No. 7F

Within three days of the victory at New Market, Gen. Robert E. Lee ordered Breckinridge to move the majority of his force to Spotsylvania to reinforce him, leaving only a guard to watch over the Valley. On May 19, in Staunton, Breckinridge's men boarded trains bound for Charlottesville. Within a day, they arrived at Hanover Junction, near Richmond. Though Staunton had once again been spared from the footsteps of the "invading horde," concern had to dwell in the minds of the Valley, most particularly over who would protect them from whatever threat lay next over the horizon.

TOUR NO. 6 June 1864, A Dark Day in the Shenandoah: Piedmont and the Fall of Staunton

BEGIN TOUR NO. 6 AT THE SITE OF THE Staunton Depot (Stop No. 7G) in Staunton. Refer to the maps on pages 122–125 for assistance in locating the sites on this tour. This tour is approximately 117 miles in length and includes 20 stops at historic buildings and sites.

Stop No. 7G

Staunton Depot

Within a week of his defeat at New Market, Gen. Franz Sigel was relieved of command and replaced by Maj. Gen. David Hunter. A day later, on May 22, 1864, Hunter issued marching orders to his army. Each man would carry an extra pair of shoes and socks, and one-hundred rounds of ammunition. For food, each man would be issued four pounds of hard bread and ten rations of coffee, sugar and salt. Meat would be had only by taking it from the farms in the path of the army. By May 26, Hunter's Army of approximately 12,000 men was moving through Strasburg toward Fishers Hill.

Left with the task of guarding the Shenandoah Valley, Gen. John D. Imboden prepared to counter Hunter's advance with little more than two cavalry regiments and a six-gun battery of horse artillery. By the evening of May 26, Imboden's scouts began reporting that the Federals were moving toward Staunton. At once, Imboden scrambled to assemble the local reserve forces. Among them was the local reserve artillery battery of Captain James C. Marquis, a "boy-company" made up of sixteen- and seventeen-year-old youths.

A day later, Imboden advised Gen. Robert E. Lee by telegraph. But Lee had no troops to spare for the defense of Staunton. Instead, Gen. William E. "Grumble" Jones was ordered to move up from southwest Virginia. Meanwhile, Staunton's enrollment officer, Col. Edwin G. Lee, was permitted to "impress" all and every available man, including those who worked the supply depot, to fill the ranks of the reserve companies.

By the evening of June 3, Jones' men had begun arriving at the Staunton Depot, and they were quickly put in line of march toward North River.

From the depot, proceed to corner of S. Lewis Street and turn right. Proceed for .1 miles to W. Johnson Street and turn right. Remain on this road (becomes Rt. 11/Valley Pike) for 16.6 miles. Turn right on Contentment Lane. House is approximately .2 miles down this lane.

Far left: Gen. David Hunter.
COURTESY OF THE LIBRARY OF CONGRESS

Left: Gen. Edwin G. Lee.
COURTESY OF WASHINGTON AND LEE UNIVERSITY LIBRARY

ELIZABETH GRATTAN HOUSE/ "CONTENTMENT"

STOP NO. 31

From the corner of Rt. 11 and Contentment Lane, turn left and proceed south for 2.2 miles and turn left on Rt. 994/Dice's Spring Road. Continue for 2.8 miles to Rt. 276 South/ Keezletown Road and turn right. Continue for .2 miles and turn left on Rt. 256/Weyers Cave Road. Proceed for 3.25 miles and turn right on Rt. 865/Rockfish Road. Proceed for .35 miles and turn right on Snowflake Mill Road in Mt. Meridian.

Though Jones' and Imboden's forces assembled at North River, by Saturday morning, it had become clear that Hunter was moving east toward Port Republic, thereby avoiding the Confederate force. Imboden, who was familiar with the terrain of Augusta County, proposed a defense at Mowry's Hill, between Port Republic and Staunton and within three miles of New Hope. By Saturday afternoon, Jones and Imboden halted here, just north of Augusta County and sent cavalry across Middle River toward Piedmont. Here, Jones officially assumed command of the combined forces, by this time estimated at approximately 5,600 men and twelve cannon. Jones'

The Grattan House/"Contentment."

force bivouacked for the night, but near dawn on June 5, they began to march across Middle River.

Stop No. 32 — Mt. Meridian

Gen. Julius Stahel.
Courtesy of the National Archives

While most of the 18th Virginia Cavalry spent the night a mile to the south on the Crawford Farm at "Bonnie Doon," a twenty-man picket line was established near this point to monitor Hunter's advance and sound the alarm upon being threatened. Early on Sunday morning, June 5, as Jones' columns entered Piedmont, the twenty-man detail encountered Gen. Julius Stahel's Federal cavalry here, advancing upon the Staunton Road. After a short exchange of fire, the Confederate troopers adhered to their orders not to become involved in a risky encounter and dashed off toward "Bonnie Doon."

Alarmed by the shots they heard to the north, the remaining elements of the 18th Virginia Cavalry pressed on toward Mt. Meridian to meet the oncoming bluecoats. As the 18th Virginia came onto the field, they immediately met the 1st New York (Lincoln) Cavalry and drove it back toward Port Republic. However, as the 18th continued northward and distanced itself from the main Confederate line, its position became precarious. Soon, the Lincoln Cavalry was reinforced by the 21st New York Cavalry, and the combined force countercharged, pressing the 18th back toward Mt. Meridian with heavy losses in numbers captured. Capt. Frank Imboden was among them. As more Federal cavalry entered the fray, the contest began to weigh heavily against the 18th, which was ordered to fight a delaying action until it had crossed Crawford Run. General Imboden, who led the delaying action, escaped capture by jumping his horse over a fence and dashing down a side lane toward the river.

Continue south on Rt. 865/ Rockfish Road (becomes Rt. 608/ Battlefield Road) for approximately one mile to "Bonnie Doon" (2190 Battlefield Road). The present house is a postwar structure.

Union Cavalry Charge.
From *Battles and Leaders of the Civil War*

Lt. G. Julian Pratt of the 18th Virginia Cavalry took command of Company H after Capt. Frank Imboden had been captured. Pratt would be a part of the local Confederate Veterans' movement in years after the war.
FROM *BEAUTIFUL THORNROSE: MEMORIAL EDITION*

CRAWFORD HOUSE/"BONNIE DOON" STOP NO. 33

At "Bonnie Doon" the 18th Virginia Cavalry soon found help from Major Sturgis Davis' battalion of recently activated reservists. Among Davis' men were Capt. George Chrisman's Boy Company and Capt. Henry Harnsberger's Old Man Company.

During a critical point in the fight, when the 18th Virginia was caught between the two fences that bordered the lane near "Bonnie Doon," the boys and old men of Davis' reserves charged and engaged New York cavalrymen long enough for the men of the 18th to get out of their predicament. Though the Confederates held this point against a number of Federal charges, they sustained heavy losses. Of the forty-five boys that Chrisman took into the fight, thirty were listed among the casualties. Meanwhile, Harnsberger's company was recorded to have taken over 50 percent casualties.

In short order, additional Confederate troops, including the 23rd Virginia Cavalry and two companies of Kenton Harper's Augusta Reserves came to the aid of the embattled Confederates here. However, when the Federals found a way to flank the position, the Confederates were forced to retire once again. Soon, Imboden, who could see Federal infantry moving up in support of the cavalry, called for more reinforcements.

Continue south on Rt. 608/ Battlefield Road for 1.5 miles to Rt. 776/Hatchery Road. Crawford Run meanders just to the north and south of this point.

"Bonnie Doon." From a photo taken circa 1880.
Courtesy of Rod McDonnell

Right: Postwar photo of Lt. Carter Berkeley.
FROM *A REBEL CAVALRYMAN*

Far Right: Capt. Henry A. DuPont.
COURTESY OF HAGLEY MUSEUM AND LIBRARY, WILMINGTON, DELAWARE

STOP NO. 34 — CRAWFORD RUN

Continue south on Rt. 608/ Battlefield Road for .65 miles and turn right on Rt. 774/Piedmont Road. From this point, you can look to the east and see the Shaver House that was Hunter's headquarters during the Battle of Piedmont. The right of the Confederate line is approximately .3 miles south of this point. The line is identified with an excellent stone and panel marker but does not provide safe and ample room for a pull-off that would allow time for reading about the site.

By 9 a.m., a section of Capt. John H. McClanahan's Battery of Horse Artillery arrived on the field. McClanahan's Battery, like many others on the field that day, was native to the area. As Lt. Carter Berkeley's section raced to the front, shouting and singing, through Piedmont, their progress was cheered by the ladies along the way on their porches. When within range, Berkeley planted his two guns and opened fire, halting the advance of Stahel's cavalry once again. The artillery fire kept up for a half hour until Capt. Henry A. DuPont brought up ten guns to bear down on the Confederates.

In the midst of the artillery duel, Imboden, baffled by the quick arrival of the reinforcements, rode to the rear to consult with Jones. When he discovered that the Confederate line was substantially to the north of the proposed line at Mowery's Hill, Imboden at once began to protest. In the heated discussion that ensued, Jones reminded Imboden, in rather sharp tones, that he was in command on the field, not Imboden.

STOP NO. 35 — CONFEDERATE DEFENSES AT PIEDMONT

Writing long after the battle, Capt. John Opie opined that "General Jones had selected a most miserable position. . . . Instead of occupying a line of hills, where his artillery would have full play upon the advancing enemy, he placed his army in a level woodland, where his artillery would have no sweep."

The main Confederate line was at this point, just north of Piedmont. Deploying his army in an "L" shape, anchored on a bend in the Middle River, Gen. "Grumble" Jones' army faced north. In the center of the line, Confederates had piled up the fence rails to establish a makeshift breastwork. Placing his two veteran brigades (under Col. Beuhring Jones and Col. William H. Browne) on the left and center behind barricades of fence rails, Jones positioned the reserves in the woods just to the south and west of Piedmont. Brig. Gen. John C. Vaughn's Tennessee cavalry brigade was in position along the Cross Road (present-day Route 778) east of Piedmont. Artillery support for Jones consisted of Capt. Thomas A. Bryan's Battery, Capt. John H. McClanahan's Battery of Horse Artillery, and Capt. James C. Marquis' Battery of Reserve Artillery. Having already been heavily engaged in the early morning, Imboden's cavalry was ordered behind Polecat Draft near Round Hill. The quarter-mile gap that lay between the cavalry and Jones' main line would eventually prove to be the "Achilles heel" of Jones' defense.

Postwar photo of Capt. John N. Opie.
FROM *A REBEL CAVALRYMAN*

As the Confederates settled into their positions, Generals Imboden and Jones rode along the line. Jones was gleeful, and often repeated as he passed from one command to another: "Aim low, boys, aim low, and hit'em below the belt. And be sure you see them before you shoot. Aim low and make every shot tell."

Confederate troops on the move.
FROM *BATTLES AND LEADERS OF THE CIVIL WAR*

Continue south for .3 miles and look to your left to see the battlefield marker placed here in the early twentieth century. Continue on another .4 miles to Knightly Mill Road. Note the large house (Site E) just to the southeast near the corner of the road, as this house served as a hospital after the battle. Turn around and proceed north on Rt. 608, approximately .6 miles back to Rt. 774/Piedmont Road and turn left. Proceed for .3 miles to Cline River Road.

Cornelius Shaver House. (Site D)

Gen. John C. Vaughn.
Courtesy of Mrs. Nelda Epps, Palestine, Texas

Piedmont Battlefield marker dedicated in the early twentieth century.

Also known as "Belmont," the Beard family house is one of the remaining structures in this locality that bore witness to the Battle of Piedmont and served as a temporary hospital following the battle. (Site E)

Stop No. 36 — Moor's Attack

Col. Augustus Moor.
Courtesy of the United States Army Military History Institute

After a morning of maneuvering and brushing aside dismounted Confederate cavalry, in the early afternoon Union infantry finally began to descend on the Confederate left. Leading the way was Col. Augustus Moor's brigade. When Moor's brigade arrived in front of the Confederate line, it was deployed to the right of the Staunton Road toward the river bend and it quickly met with fire from the Confederate skirmish line. Meanwhile, Col. Joseph Thoburn, whose troops had sustained heavy losses at New Market, deployed his brigade to the left of the road near the Shaver House. Though Thoburn did not receive much enemy fire, Moor, immediately in the Confederate front, took a beating. After three deadly frontal assaults, Moor called for the assistance of DuPont, who sent up two guns from Capt. Alfred Von Kleiser's Battery. When Von Kleiser opened fire, one Connecticut soldier recalled, "The very first shot made a hole through the rail pen you could drive a horse through, and the Rebs rushed out like bees swarming out of a hive."

Fire from Von Kleiser's guns devastated the ranks of the 36th Virginia Infantry. A sergeant with the 36th recalled, "That part of the regiment exposed to the enemy's fire suffered severely in killed and wounded. I saw a cannon ball strike in the midst of one of the companies, and mortally wounded several men." For a while, it appeared that the line would not hold, and General Jones made plans to withdraw to the Cross Road. However, after pushing back two Federal assaults, Jones changed his mind and altered his line slightly. Then he launched a heavy assault against Moor. This maneuver proved deadly for the Confederate defenses and revealed the gap in the center of their line, which Hunter was quick to exploit.

Return .3 miles to Rt. 608/Battlefield Road and turn right. Proceed for .7 miles to Rt. 778/Patterson Mill Road. Turn left and proceed .3 miles to a good pull-off point. Look to the north to get a perspective of the left flank of Thoburn's attack.

Stop No. 37 — Thoburn's Attack

As the fight progressed, Hunter dispatched orders to Thoburn to move up and take advantage of the gap in the Confederate line. Meanwhile, having already silenced Marquis' and McClanahan's guns, DuPont was ordered to mass the firepower from his twenty-two guns against the angle in Jones' line. Sometime before 3 p.m., Thoburn's command slipped through a ravine and woods on the right and made the fatal thrust toward Jones' right-middle flank. Realizing that his flank was compromised, Jones immediately took measures to fill the void. Harper's Reserves were among those to arrive and poured a horrific fire into the ranks of the 34th Massachusetts Infantry, felling perhaps as many as fifty men within minutes. Then, as the fight

View from the Confederate right flank in the direction of Thoburn's attack.

evolved into a horrible episode of hand-to-hand combat, both sides struggled for the right to finally win the day.

Riding from unit to unit, yelling encouragements, Jones struggled to maintain the Confederate line. Though a valiant effort was made by reserve Lt. Monroe Blue to hold the line, he was quickly singled out as a target and shot. As one Pennsylvanian later recalled, "Several of us cut loose at him and he spun around, dropped his sword, and fell to the ground." As the reserve lieutenant fell, so did any hope of rallying the men. As his line disintegrated, Jones made one last effort to rally his men, spurring his horse onward into the Federals. Within minutes, Jones lay dead on the field having taken a Minie ball to the forehead. Soon after, the defense unraveled altogether and the Confederates were routed from the field.

Return .3 miles to Rt. 608/Battlefield Road. Turn left and proceed .9 miles. Turn left at the old New Hope School to see the Virginia Civil War Trails marker (Site F). Once you have read the marker, continue south on Rt. 608 for .45 miles and turn left on Rt. 617/Round Hill School Road. Continue .1 miles to the Providence Methodist Church on the right. The modern structure has been built around part of the original church. The church served as a hospital after the battle.

Far left: Col. Joseph Thoburn. Thoburn was later mortally wounded at the Battle of Cedar Creek in October 1864.
COURTESY OF THE UNITED STATES ARMY MILITARY HISTORY INSTITUTE

Left: Gen. William E. "Grumble" Jones.
FROM *PHOTOGRAPHIC HISTORY OF THE CIVIL WAR*

Stop No. 38 — Providence Methodist Church

As Thoburn broke the Confederate right and Moor pressed down upon the Confederate center and left, Confederate soldiers were sent fleeing to the rear, and toward Middle River. Amidst the hail of Minie balls, some tumbled down the bluff and into the river. Among the many men captured at the river was Col. Beuhring Jones.

Small pockets of fighting occurred along the route from Piedmont to New Hope before the action closed for the day. General John C. Vaughn assembled what remained of the army and marched it along the East Road to Fishersville, arriving there late that night. Confederate losses for the day summed to nearly 1,500 men, while losses for Hunter's troops probably numbered closer to 900. Confederates used this church as a field hospital that night, treating both Confederate and Union soldiers.

In Staunton, Col. Edwin G. Lee summarized the day in his telegraph to General Lee: "We have been pretty badly whipped. . . . I fear Staunton will go up." Indeed, for the first time in three years, the road to Staunton lay wide open for the Union army.

On Monday morning, Vaughn began the march through Waynesboro and toward the Blue Ridge Tunnel in Rockfish Gap. Meanwhile Hunter marched south along the Staunton Road, through New Hope and to a fork in the road where he decided, instead of moving on Waynesboro and finishing the Confederates, to march on to Staunton where he would unite with Crook who was advancing toward Buffalo Gap.

The timing of the victory at Piedmont was fortuitous in that it coincided with the Republican Convention being held in Baltimore; there is no doubt that it helped in some way to solidify support for Lincoln in his run for a second term in office.

Return to Rt. 608 and turn left. Proceed for 1.3 miles and turn right onto Rt. 786/Eakle Road.

Stop No. 39 — The March to Staunton

With faith in themselves restored and in jubilant spirits, Union soldiers set off toward Staunton on June 6. As one soldier put it: "We took up our line of march, feeling as happy as a big sunflower." Along the path of the army, soldiers encountered several displays of support. Before reaching the village of Piedmont, a local raised the Stars and Stripes atop his log hut, only to be greeted by "cheer after cheer" from along the Union line of march. Further along the route, Federals were warmly welcomed. Thoburn wrote that "on the way from Piedmont

Col. David H. Strother, also known as the artist "Porte Crayon."
COURTESY OF THE UNITED STATES ARMY MILITARY HISTORY INSTITUTE

here we found about one half of the families who gave evidence of sympathy and good will toward us." Thoburn concluded that "if proper rule was exercised over the people of this country, one half of them would be outspoken friends of the Union."

Col. David H. Strother was also surprised by the local displays of appreciation. "The people along the route were either very much frightened or very glad to see us." Some "waved their handkerchiefs, such as they had them, and brought buckets of water and milk" while "a dozen or more girls in their Sunday dresses stood by the roadside in front of the cottage and presented us with bouquets."

Continue on Rt. 786 for 2.3 miles and turn right on Rt. 839/Eureka Mill Road. Continue for .55 miles and turn right on Rt. 254/Hermitage Road. Proceed for 2.1 miles and turn left on Rt. 254/New Hope Road. Proceed 2.2 miles and turn left on National Road. Continue 1.2 miles and turn right on Rt. 250/Richmond Road. Proceed 1.7 miles and merge right and turn left after the railroad overpass. Proceed for .2 miles and turn left on S. Augusta Street to reach the Staunton Depot.

STAUNTON DEPOT — STOP NO. 7H

All day during the battle of June 5, the streets of Staunton were occupied by Confederates preparing to evacuate. Joseph A. Waddell noted that "diligent preparations for departure in case of disaster were going on at the various government depots and offices. Railroad trains and wagons were loaded up, and all hands connected with the quartermaster and commissary departments were ready to start at a moments warning." Late in the day, news had swept into town of the death of General Jones and the collapse of the Confederate army. "The army wagon trains and many citizens immediately left the town, going up the Greenville road and crossing the Blue Ridge into Nelson County at Tye River Gap."

Though a Federal cavalry force had encountered light Confederate resistance in Staunton, the main body of Hunter's army marched on

"Reception in Staunton" by Porte Crayon. While local slaves were put to work tearing up the railroad tracks at Staunton, one local noted that they went about the work in half-hearted fashion as they knew that once the Federals left the town, the slaves would be put to work restoring the damage they had inflicted.
FROM *VIRGINIA ILLUSTRATED*

without much concern. Seeking a grand entrance to what had been for three years, the unreachable "Gibraltar" of the Shenandoah Valley, Colonel Strother gathered two bands with a large American flag to accompany Hunter's staff as they entered the town. "We made our tour of the principal streets playing 'Hail Columbia' and 'Yankee Doodle' and other such airs as we thought might be useful and pleasing to the inhabitants. A few skinny, sallow women peeped from between the half-closed window blinds, but generally the houses were closed and the town looked frightened. The staff dismounted at the American Hotel."

Despite the hardships of war, the Union soldiers still took time to take in the beauty of the town upon arriving. A member of a Connecticut regiment wrote that "the scenery in this vicinity is grand." Likewise, one Pennsylvanian noted, "Tis a beautiful place. The roses are in bloom; so many flowers."

From the depot, continue to S. Lewis Street and turn right. Proceed for .12 miles and turn right on W. Beverley Street. Proceed for .1 miles and turn right on Augusta Street. The old *Spectator* office was located opposite of Barrister Row, at 10 S. Augusta Street, which is now part of the bank parking lot.

STOP NO. 40 — SITE OF THE *SPECTATOR* OFFICE

One of the first places visited by Hunter's staff was the office of the *Staunton Spectator.* As Colonel Strother and Lt. Col. Charles G. Halpine approached the office, Richard Mauzy, the paper's editor and owner, sat upon the steps with a local Presbyterian minister. Greeting Mauzy, the officers asked if they could enter and inspect the shop. Also, they asked if they could have some printing done, and they indicated that they would pay for such work. Mauzy had no printers in the office, however, as most of them had been taken earlier into the ranks of General Jones' makeshift army prior to Piedmont. In the end, because Strother and Halpine were literary men, Mauzy was able to secure a note of protection and a guard for the office.

Despite the order of protection, as the Federal army withdrew on June 7, so too departed the guard posted at the door. In a short while, as Mauzy recalled, "There came, tramp, tramp, and about twenty rough-

Far left: Col. Charles G. Halpine.
COURTESY OF THE UNITED STATES ARMY MILITARY HISTORY INSTITUTE

Left: Richard Mauzy.
FROM THE *AUGUSTA HISTORICAL BULLETIN*

looking soldiers, who halted at the office and proceeded to enter, when I asked them what they wanted. They said they wanted to enter; when I told them I had the key, and at the same time showed the leader the protection given me. He glanced at it casually, and in a rough tone remarked: 'I have different orders from that, sir.' And in they rushed on their mission of destruction."

After the Federals had torn apart the office, they made their way to Charley Cochran's tobacco store on West New Street, south of Beverley and helped themselves to the "pipes, tobacco, etc, and had not the politeness to thank him . . . 'like the boy the calf ran over, had nothing to say,' his feeling being inexpressible."

Continue along Augusta Street toward the Staunton Depot. American Hotel is on the left near the depot.

AMERICAN HOTEL — STOP NO. 41A

Though Hunter made his headquarters in the Virginia Hotel, he directed prominent locals demanding an audience to Colonel Strother at the American Hotel. Here, Strother met with Mayor N. K. Trout and other members of the town council, with Alexander H. H. Stuart as well as the superintendent of the "lunatic asylum," the principal of the Wesleyan Female Institute and several other prominent men of Staunton. While these leaders urged that private property be protected, Strother made it clear that he would adhere to the policies of "warring according to the rules of civilized nations." Further, he would ensure that all military stores be confiscated and all manufacturing buildings, shops, and storehouses devoted to the war effort be destroyed. Private schools and charitable institutions would be protected, however. Strother did point out that "disorders might take place such as were to be expected among an ill-disciplined soldiery, but . . . no pains would be spared to keep peace and order in the town."

Modern view of American Hotel.

Western Virginia Lunatic Asylum, Staunton. (Site K)
FROM THE HAMRICK COLLECTION

Destruction of some buildings began that afternoon and, by Tuesday, most of the burnings were under way. According to one historian, "Public buildings were burned to the ground—railroad depots, the Confederate workshop on Lewis and Frederick Streets, the steam mill on the Middlebrook Road, Crawford and Young's woolen factory, J. I. A. Trotter's two stables near the railroad underpass and on Market Street, the steam distillery, the enormous tax-in-kind storehouse on Main Street, a foundry, and the forage houses." Perhaps as much as $500,000 worth of property was destroyed.

According to Strother, Francis T. Stribling, superintendent of the lunatic asylum (Site K), saved that institution by informing the Federals that the Confederates had placed stores of goods in the asylum. Federals seized the goods but spared the buildings.

Continue past the Staunton Depot to S. Lewis Street and turn right. Continue .25 miles and turn left on W. Frederick Street. Proceed for .45 miles to Beverley Street. Turn right and proceed for .4 miles and turn left on Straith Street. Proceed 2.7 miles and turn left on Rt. 693/Cedar Green Road. After .1 miles, turn right on Rt. 703/Hebron Road. Hebron Church is approximately 1 mile on the right.

Right: Staunton Mayor Nicholas K. Trout.
FROM *BEAUTIFUL THORNROSE, 1907*

Far right: Col. Rutherford B. Hayes of the 23rd Ohio Infantry was one of two future U.S. presidents among the occupying Union forces in Staunton in June 1864. Hayes' assistant quartermaster was future President William McKinley.
FROM *GENERALS IN BLUE*/WARNER COLLECTION

Far left: Gen. William L. "Mudwall" Jackson, second cousin to Gen. Stonewall Jackson.
FROM *GERNERALS IN GRAY*/ THE WARNER COLLECTION

Left: Gen. John C. McCausland.
COURTESY OF WEST VIRGINIA DIVISION OF CULTURE AND HISTORY.

HEBRON CHURCH

STOP NO. 42

By noon on June 7, Hunter's army began moving out of Staunton toward Buffalo Gap, in an attempt to link up with Crook who reportedly was moving in that direction. The Federals anticipated mild resistance as they marched west from Staunton.

Although Federal cavalry did come upon a site that had served as a Confederate cavalry camp, near Hebron Church, no resistance was met. Col. William L. "Mudwall" Jackson's Confederate cavalry brigade had been active in the area; it had arrived near Buffalo Gap around June 5 but had since moved to Middlebrook where it joined Col. John McCausland's brigade on June 6. Up until the arrival of Hunter's men, Jackson had kept busy by delaying Crook's advance, having fallen back through Millboro Springs, Panther's Gap, Goshen, and Craigsville.

Taking the Parkersburg Turnpike, Hunter's army moved a short distance out of Staunton before turning onto a side road leading to Hebron Church and Swoope. A member of the 22nd Pennsylvania Cavalry noted that once they had arrived at Hebron Church, they found that Jackson had "skedaddled, except a few of his men, who fled at our approach."

After destroying two nearby railroad bridges, the Federal cavalry, along with the columns of infantry, returned to Staunton and drove out a small Confederate cavalry force that had slipped in along the Middlebrook Road.

While a link-up between Hunter and Crook had not yet occurred, sometime during the day of Hunter's arrival at Hebron Church, Crook had crossed North Mountain, camping that evening at Middlebrook.

From Hebron Church, retrace your route 1 mile to Rt. 693/Cedar Green Road and turn right. Proceed for 1.9 miles and turn left on Rt. 252/Middlebrook Road. Continue 1.9 miles and turn right on Rt. 262 East. After 2 miles, merge right onto Rt. 11 North. Proceed for .3 miles and turn right on Rt. 644/Frontier Drive. Proceed 1.8 miles and turn right on Rt. 250 East/Richmond Road. Proceed for 9.8 miles to the corner of Main Street and Wayne Avenue in Waynesboro.

On June 8, Crook finally arrived with his army in Staunton.

In the Middlebrook area, Crook's men wasted no time in seizing personal items, destroying the Mish family home known as "Hillcrest" as well as destroying the Joseph T. Mitchell house at "Fairmont Farms."

Stop No. 43a

Waynesboro

As Federals made short work of Confederate depot supplies and buildings in Staunton, Federal cavalry was sent toward Waynesboro to ascertain the whereabouts of the remaining Confederate forces. Though Vaughn had taken refuge in the Blue Ridge following the Battle of Piedmont, reinforcements were arriving on a regular basis. McCausland and Jackson had already arrived, and Gen. John C. Breckinridge was on his way from Lee's army near Richmond.

From the corner of Main Street and Wayne Avenue in Waynesboro, continue east for .7 miles and turn right on Delphine Avenue (becomes Rt. 664/Mt. Torry Road after a distance). Continue 10.9 miles to the remains of Mt. Torry Furnace.

Though Federal cavalry had probed toward Waynesboro since June 7, on June 9, when they finally entered the town, they encountered heavy resistance from Gen. John D. Imboden's cavalry. The 15th New York Cavalry lost several men in the engagement. Before they retired, however, the Federals destroyed part of the railroad in town.

Later that night, Hunter's plans were altered. Instead of marching on Charlottesville, the combined Federal armies would continue south to Lexington and then would strike Lynchburg from the west.

Late nineteenth century view of the town of Waynesboro, appearing much as it probably appeared in 1864.
From *Waynesboro Days of Yore*

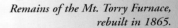

Remains of the Mt. Torry Furnace, rebuilt in 1865.

Mt. Torry Furnace

Stop No. 44

Within a day of the hard skirmish at Waynesboro, Hunter's Federal army including the commands of Crook and William W. Averell, was on the move. Meanwhile, Gen. A. N. Duffie, commanding Hunter's division of cavalry, moved toward Waynesboro, searching for gaps across the Blue Ridge that would lead to the headwaters of the Tye River. The Federals met little resistance at Waynesboro and drove in the small Confederate picket that stood in front of the town. Moving on toward the Tye River, Duffie inadvertently came upon Mt. Torry Furnace. Though unplanned, the discovery of the furnace was an added bonus to the expedition.

Named for nearby Torry Ridge, this iron ore furnace was built circa 1804. Rebuilt in 1853, by the time of the Civil War the furnace was an important source of iron for the Confederacy. According to the records of Richmond's Tredegar Iron Works, the site employed at least fifty-five slaves and free blacks and twenty white men and forty animals.

Immediately after arriving at the furnace on that warm June afternoon, the Federals went to work, destroying the furnace and breaking up the machinery. Food and forage supplies were also destroyed. Imboden's cavalry continued to pursue, but it was only able to skirmish with Duffie's rearguard.

Mt. Torry was rebuilt by January of 1865, but the new machinery, manufactured at Tredegar shops in Richmond, had yet to be set up.

Gen. Alfred Napoleon Alexander Duffie.
From *Photographic History of the Civil War*

From Mt. Torry Furnace, turn around and proceed north along Rt. 664/Mt. Torry Road for 8.6 miles and turn onto Interstate 64 West. Continue approximately 10 miles toward Staunton. Merge left toward I-81 South and take exit 220/Rt. 262 West. This will take you to Rt. 11 North. Turn right on Rt. 11 North/Lee-Jackson Highway. Proceed 1.2 miles and turn left on Ritchie Boulevard. Proceed .1 miles and turn right on Charles Street. Proceed approximately .1 miles to the site of "Gaymont" (now the location of headquarters of the Potomac Conference of Seventh-Day Adventists).

Gen. Joseph R. Anderson.
FROM *PHOTOGRAPHIC HISTORY OF THE CIVIL WAR*

Equipped by J. R. Anderson, owner and ironmaster of the blast furnaces at the Tredegar foundry, the new Mt. Torry would be equipped with cylinders made of iron instead of wood. The modification increased capacity from 1,200 to 1,500 tons. Mt. Torry operated until well into the twentieth century.

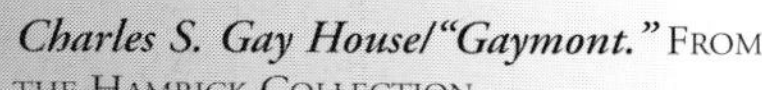

Charles S. Gay House/"Gaymont." FROM THE HAMRICK COLLECTION

Site of the Charles Scott Gay House/"Gaymont"

Stop No. 45

As Duffie struck out toward the Tye River, the bulk of Hunter's command divided: one portion took the Middlebrook Road while the other took to the Valley Turnpike. As the Federal forces moved toward Lexington, small bands of Confederates quickly descended on Staunton to gather Union stragglers. Several of Hunter's wounded had been left at the Confederate General Hospital. Meanwhile, along the routes of travel taken by the Federal troops, small bands of Confederate cavalry harassed the Federals and attempted to impede their forward progress. The Confederates stirred up minor skirmishes at Middlebrook, Newport, and Midway (June 11) with little result.

Here, at the Charles Scott Gay home known as "Gaymont," Federal soldiers camped in the front field shortly after having moved out of Staunton. As Confederates quickly moved into Staunton and occupied Sears Hill, Mrs. Gay, fearing that hostilities might follow on her property, wanted to move her family to the safety of the Deaf and Blind School. She requested to meet with General Hunter but was unable to do so. Ultimately, with the speed of the departing Federal army and the light number of Confederates actually camped on Sears Hill, nothing came of her concerns.

Return to Greenville Avenue and turn left. Proceed .45 miles and turn left on E. Hampton Street (as you travel along this road, you will cross Sears Hill, mentioned in the story of Gaymont). Proceed .25 miles and turn left on Rt. 252/Middlebrook Road. Continue for 9.1 miles and turn left on Rt. 701/Howardsville Road. Proceed for approximately 1.8 miles. The James Bumgardner Jr. House/ "Bethel Green" will be on the right. It is suggested that you pull off to the left in the church parking lot.

James Bumgardner Jr. House/ "Bethel Green"

Stop No. 46

Built circa 1850, this was the home of the James Bumgardner family. In June 1864, as Hunter's men marched through the area, a part of the army camped on this farm. Alone and apprehensive of the "Yankees," the women of the house feared for their property. However, as fortune would have it, one of the Federal captains in the group was a prewar acquaintance of the family and gave orders that the house be left alone.

James Bumgardner Jr. is seen in the photo of the officers of the West Augusta Guard, along with W. S. H. Baylor, in Tour No. 1 of this book. Born in Fayette, Howard County, Missouri, in 1835, he and his family moved to Virginia in 1847. A graduate of Brownsburg Academy, James attended the University of Virginia from 1852 to 1853 and returned to Staunton where he served as a clerk, a lawyer, and a schoolteacher. A lieutenant in the West Augusta Guard from 1858 to 1861, Bumgardner, at the opening of the war, enlisted in Company L of the 5th Virginia Infantry. By August 1862,

James Bumgardner Jr. House/ "Bethel Green."

Bumgardner had attained the rank of captain. Captured at the Battle of Third Winchester/Opequon on September 19, 1864, he remained as a prisoner of war in Fort Delaware until June 1865. After the war, Bumgardner served as commonwealth's attorney for Augusta County (1866–1888), captain of the local Virginia Militia (1871), and was a member (and commander, 1901–1902) of the Stonewall Jackson Camp Confederate Veterans in Staunton. He died September 2, 1917, and was buried in the Bethel Presbyterian Church Cemetery, near where you are now parked.

From Bethel Presbyterian Church, turn back 1.8 miles to Middlebrook Road and turn left. Continue for 1.5 miles to the corner of Cherry Grove Road and Middlebrook Village Road in the heart of the village of Middlebrook.

Stop No. 47

Middlebrook

The village of Middlebrook and several of the buildings still standing bore witness to the advance of Federal soldiers on their way to Lexington in June 1864. As elements of Confederate cavalry stood in the path of the Federals, a minor skirmish also took place here.

At various points between Staunton and the nearby Augusta/ Rockbridge County line, soldiers left a wake of destruction and vandalism, well remembered by locals.

At the home of Brook Eskridge, at "Woodlands Farm," five miles south of Staunton on the Valley Pike, Federal soldiers ran pell-mell all over the property. Though the family had hidden the hams and silver

Early twentieth-century view of Middlebrook.
From the Hamrick Collection

under the floors, the bluecoats destroyed what they could find and hauled away a number of other family items as well.

Just to the east, near Mint Spring, the Alex Gardner House, known as "Locust Lawn," also fell prey to the Federals. At one time during the march, a number of Federals broke ranks and fired through the door and into the dining room, and raided the house of its foodstuffs.

From Middlebrook, continue for 2.5 miles. Locust Grove will be on the right.

John Sproul House/ "Locust Grove"

Stop No. 48

While many farmers had taken their livestock out of the area in fear of depredations at the hands of enemy soldiers, at the nearby John Sproul farm of "Locust Grove," Federals were surprised at what they saw. As they marched along the road, a flock of sheep grazed quietly in a field beside the road and even jumped in front of and between the line of troops headed toward Lexington.

As the Federals made their way past the property, the family was forced to take in two Union soldiers who were suffering from typhoid fever. One of the soldiers died. However, while the buildings of the farm may have been spared from destruction, the family would not be spared from the typhoid dysentery. In mid-August, John and Matilda

John Sproul House/"Locust Grove."

Sproul lost two children and a nephew: Matilda (age 30), her brother and former colonel of the 93rd Virginia Militia, William S. Sproul (age 36), and a nephew, James Bumgardner Sproul (age 4). The family also lost four slaves to the deadly disease.

Within exactly one week of leaving Staunton, and in the wake of destruction left from Augusta County to Lexington and beyond, Hunter advanced on Lynchburg. As he initiated his attacks, however, Hunter was thwarted by the remarkably well-timed arrival by rail of Gen. Jubal Early's Second Corps, from the Army of Northern Virginia. On June 18, Hunter began to withdraw, back across the Blue Ridge and through West Virginia. With the Union forces that threatened the Valley well occupied in the wake of the disaster at Lynchburg, Early took the opportunity to mount an attack into Maryland and against the defenses within sight of Washington, D.C. Having failed at Lynchburg, at his own request, Hunter was relieved of command in August 1864. Hunter was replaced by Gen. Philip H. Sheridan, a man possessed of significantly more determination.

TOUR NO. 7 — September 26–29, 1864, Second Occupation of Staunton, Waynesboro and the Battle for the Bridge

BEGIN TOUR NO. 7 AT THE SITE OF THE Samuel Cline House (Stop No. 49A) in Verona. Refer to the maps on pages 122–125 for assistance in locating the sites on this tour. This tour is approximately 44 miles in length and includes 6 stops at historic buildings and sites.

Following his raid into Maryland and after bringing his force against the defenses of Washington, D.C., Early withdrew back into the Shenandoah Valley where he successfully engaged Federal forces on numerous occasions, from Cool Spring (July 18) to Rutherford's Farm (July 20) and Second Kernstown (July 24). With the arrival of Sheridan in the Shenandoah, however, the tables began to turn against Early. At the Battle of Third Winchester/Opequon (September 19) and Fishers Hill (September 21 and 22), Early was defeated in two engagements that cost him nearly 5,000 casualties. While the Federal casualties were comparable, Sheridan, like Grant, knew that resources were available to him, but not to Early.

Additionally, like Grant, Sheridan continued to keep the pressure on his opponent. Within days, Sheridan was in Harrisonburg, sending his cavalry out to probe toward Port Republic and Brown's Gap, where Early was held up in a defensive position. Anticipating reinforcements from the Army of Northern Virginia, Early hoped to go on the offensive again soon. In the meantime, the road to Staunton, for the second time in 1864 and the second time during the entire war, was open to the Union army.

THE SAMUEL CLINE HOUSE — STOP NO. 49A

With orders to destroy the Virginia Central Railroad lines between Staunton and Waynesboro, James H. Wilson's 3rd Division and Charles R. Lowell's Reserve Brigade, all under Gen. A. T. A. Torbert, set off from Harrisonburg at 5 a.m. on September 26.

Gen. Jubal Early.
COURTESY OF THE LIBRARY OF CONGRESS

From the corner of Rt. 11 and Bald Rock Road in Verona, proceed south for 3 miles to the fork and take the left fork in the road. Proceed for 6 miles (this road becomes Greenville Avenue/E. Johnson Street) and turn left on S. Augusta Street to the Staunton Depot.

Arriving here at the Cline House before noon, Torbert reined up in front of the house and called out to Samuel Cline, "Can you give a hungry man a bite to eat?" Wisely, Cline replied that he would be willing to feed anyone, no matter the uniform, as long as the food held out. Soon a substantial meal was set on the table, freshly prepared by Cline's wife and daughters. Before leaving the house they thanked the Clines, and one officer commented that they "would not mind soldiering if we could get a dinner like that every day." To return the favor of the dinner, Torbert left a note of protection for the property in the hands of Mr. Cline. Many of Cline's neighbors were not so fortunate. Soon, the Clines could see smoke, from several barns and mills in the area, drifting in the pleasant fall afternoon sky.

Not long after Torbert's departure, another group of Federal cavalry arrived at the house and prepared to put Cline's mill to the torch. When Samuel's son, Cyrus, asked a Federal officer why they were burning up the surrounding property, he replied, "You rebels burnt Chambersburg." Samuel was able to stop the detachment by showing them Torbert's note; his men, now called off, looked to the possibility of burning the barn across the river. Cline, being a good neighbor, told the Federals that the man who owned the property was a noncombatant and that the soldiers would scare to death the ladies who remained. Fortunately, the soldiers left that property alone as well and moved farther along the turnpike toward Staunton.

Samuel Cline House.

Far left: Gen. Philip H. Sheridan.
COURTESY OF THE NATIONAL ARCHIVES

Left: Gen. Alfred T. A. Torbert.
FROM *PHOTOGRAPHIC HISTORY OF THE CIVIL WAR*

STAUNTON DEPOT — STOP NO. 71

Two nights before the arrival of the Union horsemen, General Early had sent orders to evacuate Staunton. According to local resident and historian Joseph A. Waddell, "During that night there was little rest or sleep to persons connected with the various government depots, and as early as possible the next day all army stores were started eastward by railroad and wagon trains."

On Monday evening, September 26, Torbert's men entered Staunton and set to work. "We have been at work nearly all day destroying commissary and quartermaster stores of the Rebels and the Rail road," wrote a Federal cavalryman. "The Johnnies must have left here in a hurry as they left a deal of stuff for us to destroy. They had a large Boot and Shoe factory here which we burned. 150 dollars in Confederate Scrip is the price of a common pair of cowhide boots."

Of the brief occupation, Waddell recalled that the Federals "entered very few houses and committed no depredations of any consequence. They impressed all the negro men into their service, and took them down the railroad to destroy the track and bridges. The colored people were very indignant, and did less damage to the railroad than they could have done."

Torbert reported that, in Staunton, his men had destroyed or captured "300 muskets, 75 sabers, 50 cartridge boxes, 70 sets horse equipment, 60 rounds fixed ammunition, 200 sets harness, 350 saddle trees, 200 tents, 65 head of beef cattle, 57 prisoners, 25 wagons, 5 tons salt, 100 barrels flour, 500 bales hay, 1,000 bushels wheat, 125 barrels hard bread, 50 boxes tobacco, 50 horses, medical supplies, & etc."

From the depot continue to S. Lewis and turn right. Proceed .1 miles and turn right on W. Johnson Street. Continue on Rt. 11 North 12.3 miles and turn right on Rt. 256/Weyers Cave Road. Proceed for 2.1 miles to Rt. 773/Cave View Road.

Right: Gen. Wesley Merritt.
COURTESY OF THE NATIONAL ARCHIVES

Far right: Gen. Williams C. Wickham.
FROM *GENERALS IN GRAY*/
WARNER COLLECTION

STOP NO. 50

WEYERS CAVE ACTION

While Torbert and his command focused on Staunton before moving east toward Waynesboro, Gen. Wesley Merritt was sent toward Port Republic to "occupy the enemy's attention." Gen. Williams C. Wickham's Brigade, located at Patterson's Mill on the South River, monitored the movements of the Federals at Port Republic and Weyers Cave. Under the cover of thick foliage along the South River, Wickham moved his brigade across the South River and turned north, immediately bringing the brigade in line. After placing the 4th and 3rd Virginia Cavalry in the center and the 1st and 2nd Virginia Cavalry on the flanks, a premature cannonade by the Confederate horse artillery alerted the Federals in their camp. Having lost the opportunity for a surprise attack at Weyers Cave, Wickham's Brigade was left with no alternative but to chase after the already fleeing foe. Charging down the road from Mt. Horeb, the 4th, 3rd, and 1st Virginia drove the enemy to Mt. Meridian.

Continue along Rt. 256 East/Weyers Cave Road for 4.6 miles and turn right on Rt. 340 South. Continue for 14.4 miles and turn right on Rt. 250 West. Merge right on E. Broad Street. Continue .6 miles to Willow Oak Plaza Shopping Center. The Gallaher home, "Rose Hall," once stood near the center of the modern plaza.

STOP NO. 27B

SITE OF THE HUGH GALLAHER HOUSE/"ROSE HALL"

Early on the morning of September 28, Mrs. Gallaher called at Torbert's headquarters and asked for a safe guard, "saying her husband owned a great deal of property there and that he was a Union man who had had to 'refugee' and was then in Philadelphia, and she gave the name of the hotel he was stopping at." After breakfast, Capt. Charles Henry Veil and another cavalryman rode toward Waynesboro and found "Rose Hall" to be, "a nice brick residence." Veil posted a guard at the property with instructions to prevent any destruction or intrusion. Later that afternoon, on assignment to destroy a "large tannery and the contents of a flour mill in town," Veil set off on his task only to discover that both were owned by Mrs. Gallaher. Veil recalled that he told her what his instructions were, and "she raised no objections and I proceeded to execute them. I found the tannery full of leather being tanned in the vats and a warehouse with probably a hundred barrels of unslaked lime. As I knew a little something about tanning, I had a barrel or two of lime emptied into the vats with leather in the liquor or tan and I am pretty well I 'fixed that.' The mill had probably five hundred barrels of flour. After the command had all that it could use and I had distributed all the Negroes could carry away, I had the balances rolled out and the heads of the barrels knocked in and scattered over the ground."

The following March, when the Federals were again in town, Mrs. Gallaher sent word ahead to the Federal command, with whom Veil still rode, and invited him to "Rose Hall" for tea.

From the shopping center, turn left on Rt. 250 West/Broad Street and proceed .5 miles to East Avenue and turn right. Proceed to the corner of East and Main Street.

Postwar photo of Charles Henry Veil.
COURTESY OF THE UNITED STATES ARMY MILITARY HISTORY INSTITUTE

EAST BANK OF THE SOUTH RIVER — STOP NO. 51

After their unsuccessful escapade at Weyers Cave, Wickham's Brigade continued to operate along the western edge of the Blue Ridge. Early on September 28, the brigade crossed the South Fork and rode upriver toward Waynesboro to attack Federal cavalry that they knew had entered the town recently. As the Confederates got within a half mile of the Federal pickets, they recrossed the river to the eastern bank. Remaining as quiet as possible, the men prepared for another surprise attack. The 4th Virginia Cavalry was placed on the road leading into Waynesboro while the 2nd and 3rd Virginia were positioned to

The railroad tunnels running through the Blue Ridge were among the key objectives of the Federal cavalry in September 1864. However, the Confederate cavalry was successful in keeping the tunnels safe. FROM THE HAMRICK COLLECTION

From the corner of East and Main Street, turn right on E. Main and continue .1 miles and turn right at the Pavilion at Constitution Park.

support the charge. The 1st Virginia, among which was a company of the local boys of Waynesboro (the "Valley Rangers"), was dismounted and marched along the railroad tracks on the right. By sometime after 2 p.m., the brigade had advanced as far as the Charlottesville and Waynesboro Road, placing them about a mile from the village. Col. Thomas T. Munford noted that "we had to wait a little time for our artillery to come up. The blind road was filled with fallen trees and logs. . . ." When well up, the 1st Virginia Cavalry was dismounted and sent down the railroad toward Waynesboro and the bridge over the Shenandoah.

Col. Thomas T. Munford.
COURTESY OF THE LIBRARY OF CONGRESS

West Bank of the South River Stop No. 52

On the afternoon of September 28, while detachments of Federal horsemen went to work destroying the iron railroad bridge and burning the railroad depot and government buildings at Waynesboro, Capt. George N. Bliss, of Company H, 1st Rhode Island Cavalry, watched over the men to ensure no looting occurred that day. Plans also remained on tap to destroy the Blue Ridge tunnel in Rockfish Gap, which would render the Virginia Central Railroad out of the Valley entirely useless to Lee near Richmond. According to Bliss, "It was a perfect day of early autumn. The clear spring waters and pure air of the beautiful mountain valley had restored me to my usual perfect health."

Sometime near 3 p.m., Bliss heard shots ring out in the distance, east of the river. Looking in that direction, he saw Confederate forces driving toward the bridge. With his command of no more than a dozen men, Bliss formed a line across Main Street while Col. Charles R. Lowell ordered his men to form a skirmish line. However, Lowell's men were totally surprised—their horses were unbridled and grazing near the river and they were soon overrun. As the Confederate horse artillery barked out its first rounds against Lowell's left flank, the 4th Virginia had dashed across the bridge and found itself in the midst of the enemy.

Though this is the modern railroad bridge across the South River at Waynesboro, it runs nearly the same line as the railroad during the Civil War. Federal cavalry was unsuccessful in destroying bridges here and across Christians Creek, toward Staunton.

A Confederate cavalry charge.
FROM *BATTLES AND LEADERS OF THE CIVIL WAR*

From the Pavilion, turn right on Main Street and proceed .2 miles and turn right on Wayne Avenue. Proceed a short distance and turn left on Spring Lane.

Riding into town the men of the 4th were quickly upon those of the 1st Rhode Island Cavalry on Main Street. Captain Moss of Company K wrote that "I charged with my squadron and met . . . a regiment near a house on the right of the street near the top of a hill, in Waynesborough." After a brief but fierce skirmish, the Federals withdrew back through town to a hill that ran along its western edge.

Col. (later General) Charles Russell Lowell was later mortally wounded at the Battle of Cedar Creek in October 1864.
FROM *PHOTOGRAPHIC HISTORY OF THE CIVIL WAR*

STOP NO. 53

SPRING LANE/SITE OF CAPTAIN BLISS' CAPTURE

As the 4th Virginia Calvary removed the debris that the enemy had strewn across the road, the Federals regrouped along the western ridge. An officer of the 3rd New Jersey ordered his men forward, but the New York troopers refused the order, having seen how badly their fellow soldiers had been beaten. Furious over the attitude of his men,

Captain Bliss ordered a countercharge and dashed headlong into the 4th Virginia alone; his men did not follow.

Colonel Lowell, however, did choose to join Bliss, and he advanced with a small number of men until he realized the futility of the effort. Bliss continued on, nonetheless, unaware that he was now alone. Swinging his saber "madly from right to left," Bliss soon found himself in the midst of the Black Horse Troop. Before he took to what is believed to be this alley, the Union officer wounded four men, including a captain and a color bearer. Two other officers barely escaped Bliss' rage by ducking his swinging blade. Finally cornered in the alley and his horse shot, Bliss was sabred across the forehead and struck by the butt of a carbine before he cried out to surrender. Already infuriated at his wounding of their comrades, the enraged Virginians did not yet yield and struck Bliss yet again before a revolver was leveled at him. Fearing he was to be killed, Bliss called out for protection as a Freemason. By this time, many members of the 4th Virginia had ridden up to the scene. As they looked on, a fellow Mason soon stepped up and saved Bliss from certain death.

Soon after, the town was cleared of the Federals, and near dusk, Gen. John Pegram's infantry arrived, with supporting artillery, that gave a few parting shots into the Federal flank as the force retired out of range.

The following day, General Early held Waynesboro while Wickham rode to Staunton to monitor Sheridan's activities, but Sheridan had already pulled out. As rain began to fall that evening, Confederate cavalry set up a picket line from Staunton back to Middle River. During the next day, cavalry rode along back roads to discern the Federal troop movements.

TOUR NO. 8 September 26–October 1, 1864, The Burning

BEGIN TOUR NO. 8 AT THE SITE OF THE Patrick House "Locust Isle" (Stop No. 54) just off of Rt. 865/Rockfish Road in northeast Augusta County. Refer to the maps on pages 122–125 for assistance in locating the sites on this tour. This tour is approximately 45 miles in length and includes 8 stops at historic buildings and sites.

While destruction of rail lines, government buildings, and supplies were ordered as part of the second occupation of Augusta County, Sheridan's orders to Torbert's men were also explicit in that they would "burn all barns and mills on their route." Beginning with the burnings along the Middle River on September 26, the Federal depredations upon the civilian population continued in Augusta County through September 30.

Stop No. 54 — Patrick Family House/ "Locust Isle"

One of the first homes near Waynesboro to come under the torch was the Patrick place at "Locust Isle." The owner of "Locust Isle," William Patrick, had served as captain of the "Valley Rangers" of Waynesboro in 1861, but by 1862 he had been elevated to the rank of major and given command of the 17th Battalion Virginia Cavalry. However, by early September, and in the wake of the Second Battle of Manassas, Patrick would return to "Locust Isle" in a coffin, yet another great loss to the Augusta County community.

William Patrick Jr. in postwar years.
From *Staunton: The Queen City*

In September 1864, then, thirteen-year-old William Patrick Jr. had assumed the responsibilities as man of the house. As the Patricks possessed extensive milling and farming interests, the Federal barnburners were a serious concern. With the help of his mother, Hettie, and two younger sisters, William loaded a wagon full of family valuables and set out to distance himself from the Union army by joining a line of wagons headed out of harm's way. After a short distance, William's wagon gave way when the sickening sound of a splintering wheel split the air. With no spare wheel and without any aid from his neighbors also fleeing from Waynesboro, young Patrick

The Patrick House/"Locust Isle."

was left to his own devices, except for receiving help to get the wagon off the road.

As the last wagon of the long wagon train passed out of sight, William sat along the roadside, alone and crying, believing that Union troopers would descend upon him at any moment. Ironically, the cavalry struck farther up the road among the wagons of those who did nothing to help the youth. The Patrick family treasures had been spared.

From the Patrick House/Locust Isle, drive north on Rt. 865/Rockfish Road for 1 mile and turn left on Rt. 619/Hildebrand Church Road. Proceed 2.2 miles to Rt. 254 West/Hermitage Road. The Weade family property was somewhere nearby in the vicinity of Hermitage.

"Hermitage"/Weade Family Property — Stop No. 55

Though barns and mills had been specifically identified as the targets of Torbert's destruction, some family homes such as that of the Weade family near here, were destroyed as well. A family with large holdings of wheat and corn, the Weades became aware of the ongoing destruction and began to move furniture and other valuables out of the house and into the fields of standing corn. Though these items were spared, the family was still subject to depredations and could only look on while the Federals burned their house. Oddly, the barn and slave quarters, in which they lived during the upcoming winter, were spared.

From the corner of Rt. 619/Hildebrand Church Road and Rt. 254 West/Hermitage Road, turn right and proceed 1.2 miles and then turn left on Long Meadow Road. Proceed 3.2 miles and turn right on Emerald Hill Drive. From the corner of Long Meadow Road and Emerald Hill Drive, look to the southwest to see the David Coiner House/Long Meadows.

The David Coiner House/ "Long Meadows."

Stop No. 56

David Coiner House/ "Long Meadows"

On September 27, Susan Coiner stood with her children and sister on the portico of their house, watching the skies all around them fill with smoke from barns and mills. Susan's husband, David, had enlisted at the outset of the war with Company G, 52nd Virginia Infantry, and by that fall he was serving as 2nd sergeant. He had been wounded only a few months before at Spotsylvania Court House.

Counting no fewer than seven barns ablaze on the horizon, Susan's first thoughts were of her husband's flock of sheep, which she sought to release from the barn before the Federals arrived. No bluecoats appeared that evening, but they did arrive the next morning. Prepared to pay off the troopers with a well-hidden amount of coin money that she had been saving, Susan was surprised when the men showed no interest in burning the place, though the barn and granary were quite full from the successful crop of the year. Instead, they demanded food and forage. As the officer in charge sent his men out to the barn to look for forage, yet ordering them not to break any padlocks, he entered the home looking for food. Soon, a mulatto slave boy ran into the room and announced that the enlisted bluecoats had broken the lock on the springhouse door. Enraged, the officer headed out and scolded the men who, by then, were quite busy drinking milk directly from the stoneware crocks. The officer ordered his men to dump the milk on the ground, and it appeared that the Federals would be on their way. Observing a riding mare and her colt, the officer ordered the mare bridled and taken along. Naturally, the colt followed behind, prompting Susan to plead with the officer to leave the colt, as it would be of no use to them. The officer seemed to listen but then coldly turned to one of his men and ordered him to shoot the colt.

From the corner of Long Meadow Road and Emerald Hill Drive, turn right (north) and proceed for approximately 9 miles (becomes Rt. 608/Battlefield Road) and turn left on Rt. 774/Piedmont Road. From this point at the corner of Rt. 608 and Rt. 774, look to the northeast to see the Shaver Farm.

Cornelius Shaver Farm — Stop No. 57

Having served as the headquarters of General Hunter during the Battle of Piedmont, three months later, during the burning, the Shaver Farm would be the site of yet another episode of war in the Valley. In the wake of the June battle, Cornelius Shaver had collected a large amount of discarded debris from his fields and dumped it into a nearby swamp. Shaver's young sons, George (10) and John (6), had likewise gathered a number of relics, including several unexploded artillery shells. Using a broken sword, the boys unscrewed the unexploded shells and emptied the black powder into small sacks.

The Cornelius Shaver Farm.

With no real plans for the powder, they stored it away in the barn until they could decide what to do with it.

By the time Torbert's men, mostly men of George A. Custer's Division, arrived in this area in late September, the Shavers found themselves in the midst of a virtual hell of fires. One daughter counted perhaps a dozen fires in the surrounding area. Wasting no time at the Shaver place, the trooper dismounted and set fire to the abundance of hay and grain that filled the barn. When the fire reached the boys' stash of powder, the explosion prompted the cavalrymen to their horses and hurried them along their way. While the explosion had deterred a longer stay by the Federal cavalrymen, the powder had not been tightly packed and therefore did minimal damage. The family did have enough time to save what they could of the barn and brought enough wheat into the house to carry the family through the winter.

From the corner of Rt. 608/ Battlefield Road and Rt. 774/Piedmont Road, turn right and proceed south for 1.2 miles and turn right on Rt. 778/ Knightly Mill Road. Proceed 2.3 miles to Rt. 777/Knightly Lane. Proceed for 1 mile. The Thomas McCue House/"Belvidere" will be on the left.

The Thomas McCue House/ "Belvidere."

Thomas McCue House/ "Belvidere" — Stop No. 58

Despite the appearance that Federal troopers went about their task in an overzealous manner, many of the bluecoats, in recounting their experiences, revealed that they did not necessarily like the destructive duty they performed during the fall of 1864. A member of the 22nd Pennsylvania Cavalry wrote in his diary that it "was an unpleasant duty, but we had to obey orders." Another member of the 1st New York (Lincoln) Cavalry commented that "some men had already had enough and were willing to risk court-martial rather than continue to be agents of destruction of civilian property." Nevertheless, the troopers continued to perform their duties, creating huge sections of devastation in Augusta County.

As Federals set to work destroying the barn at "Belvidere," the nearby residence of the Thomas McCue family, Elizabeth McCue, Thomas' wife, offered the burning party $300 in gold that she had hidden in one of her slippers if they would spare their barn and house. Though the property was saved, upon mounting up to leave, one of the troopers noted a very nice broach around the neck of seventeen-year-old Bettie McCue and demanded it of her. As she handed it to the soldier, she stuck him in the finger with the pin as hard as she could. Between howls of pain, the trooper took the broach, and as he rode off he admitted that he admired the young woman's spunk.

Continue along Rt. 777/Knightly Lane for 1.75 miles to Rt. 616/Dam Town Road and turn right. Proceed .4 miles and turn right on Rt. 11 North. Proceed 4.7 miles to Burketown.

Burke's Mill — Stop No. 59

As Custer's force exited Augusta County at this point, the surrounding community was spared little. In addition to Capt. Thomas Burke's blacksmith shop, the bluecoats put the torch to David Van Pelt's merchant mill, sawmill, shingle mill, miller's house, and cooper's shop, which contained enough lumber for at least a thousand barrels. Yet another blacksmith shop was fired at B. F. Spicer's. This was followed up by the destruction of Benjamin Switzer's barn, corn house, cider press, and farming implements. As these buildings burned, the next target was in view. Just east of Burke's Mill on the North River stood Samuel Funkhouser's woolen factory. Since the mill had been known to provide woolen cloth for the Confederacy, particular attention was paid to ensure its destruction.

By the time the Federals pulled out of Augusta, like many areas yet to bear witness to similar destruction, the area around Burke's Mill

Gen. George A. Custer.
FROM *PHOTOGRAPHIC HISTORY OF THE CIVIL WAR*

Continue north on Rt. 11 for 1.3 miles and turn left on Rt. 690/Summit Church Road. Proceed for 1.6 miles to Rt. 646/Fadley Road and turn right. Continue for 2.9 miles and turn right on Rt. 42 North. Proceed .4 miles and turn left to the Mossy Creek interpretive marker.

would shed enough light so that a lantern was not necessary in the dark night that followed. In their wake, in addition to Funkhouser's Mill, Custer's troopers left afire no less than fifty barns, seven flour mills, and five sawmills.

STOP NO. 60

MOSSY CREEK IRON WORKS

While Custer's exit from the county occurred at Burke's Mill, this location marked the final spot of devastation by troopers from 3rd Cavalry Division. Here, the Federal troopers set to work destroying the Forrer family barn and some of the buildings of the Mossy Creek Iron Works. Interestingly, the furnace itself was spared. Though damage was minimal, the Forrer family had not yet seen the last of devastation at the hands of the Federals. When troopers from Col. William H. Powell's 2nd Cavalry Division entered Page County on October 1, the first structures in their path were once again iron furnaces owned by Henry Forrer. Remarkably, as with the Mossy Creek works, none of the three furnaces in Page County would be recorded as having been destroyed.

Return to Rt. 42 South. Proceed .4 miles and turn left on Rt. 646/Fadley Road. Proceed for 7.6 miles and turn right on Rt. 11 South. Continue 2.5 miles to Mt. Sidney.

Daniel Forrer House, circa 1930.
From *Christian Forrer: The Clockmaker*

When the burning ended, Torbert could account for some $3,270,650 worth of damages inflicted by his men on government and private property in Augusta County.

Mt. Sidney — Stop No. 61

By October 1, in the wake of the Federal army's withdrawal from Augusta County, Gen. Jubal Early moved his command to Mt. Sidney and took position between here and the North River. Unable to strike Sheridan while he continued his path of destruction into Rockingham, Shenandoah, and Page Counties over the next week, Early waited here at Mt. Sidney, for reinforcements to arrive. He was reinforced on October 5 by cavalry under Gen. Thomas L. Rosser, recently sent by Gen. Robert E. Lee from the Richmond defenses. By October 6, Early was ready to go on the offensive again. He had been reinforced by Rosser and an additional 2,700 muskets of Gen. Joseph Kershaw's division, as well as the guns of Col. Wilfred Cutshaw's artillery battalion. However, when he struck out toward Harrisonburg on the sixth, Early found that Sheridan was already moving back down the Valley.

Turn-of-the-century photograph of Mt. Sidney.
FROM THE HAMRICK COLLECTION

In the weeks that followed, Early would face two disastrous defeats. The Battle of Toms Brook on October 9 rendered the Confederate cavalry in the Valley relatively ineffective. However, the Battle of Cedar Creek on October 19, having the potential to have been a surprising Confederate victory, proved the end of significant Confederate resistance in the Shenandoah Valley. As winter closed in, Confederate troops as well as civilians in the Shenandoah Valley would find life to be difficult in the wake of the devastation of Sheridan's burnings.

TOUR NO. 9 December 1864–January 1865, Augusta County as Confederate Winter Quarters

BEGIN TOUR NO. 9 AT THE CORNER OF Barrenridge Road and Rt. 250 in Fishersville. The site of the 1864–1865 winter quarters for the infantry and artillery was located just to the north (Stop No. 62). Refer to the maps on pages 122–125 for assistance in locating the sites on this tour. This tour is approximately 43 miles in length and includes 9 stops at historic buildings and sites.

Following disaster at the Battle of Cedar Creek, the shattered remnants of Gen. Jubal Early's army once again retired south, up the Valley toward Harrisonburg.

As winter threatened, Early needed desperately to move his army to a position where his men could winter over and still have access to a viable supply line and transportation route to Richmond. Though they had attempted to make New Market their home for the winter, provisions in the area were scarce. The enemy lay not far down the Valley, and had ample resources to mount an attack against the Confederates at any moment. Early decided to move up the Valley to Augusta County. However, as with Shenandoah, Rockingham, and Page Counties, Augusta had not been spared destruction by Sheridan's men in October, with the consequence that rations would be an ongoing problem. A shortage of provisions, coupled with the harshness of winter weather, would contribute further to the deterioration of Early's already depleted forces. While the bulk of his army began to settle into Augusta County for the winter, Early maintained a strong cavalry presence in the Page Valley to watch both the Thornton and New Market Gaps.

Barrenridge/Infantry and Artillery Winter Quarters — Stop No. 62

Though Early's forces had begun moving into Augusta County in December, not all would remain for the winter. Soldiers of Gen. William Terry's brigade, in which also remained what was left of the grand old Stonewall Brigade, were among the first to march into Augusta County and to Waynesboro where they boarded trains bound

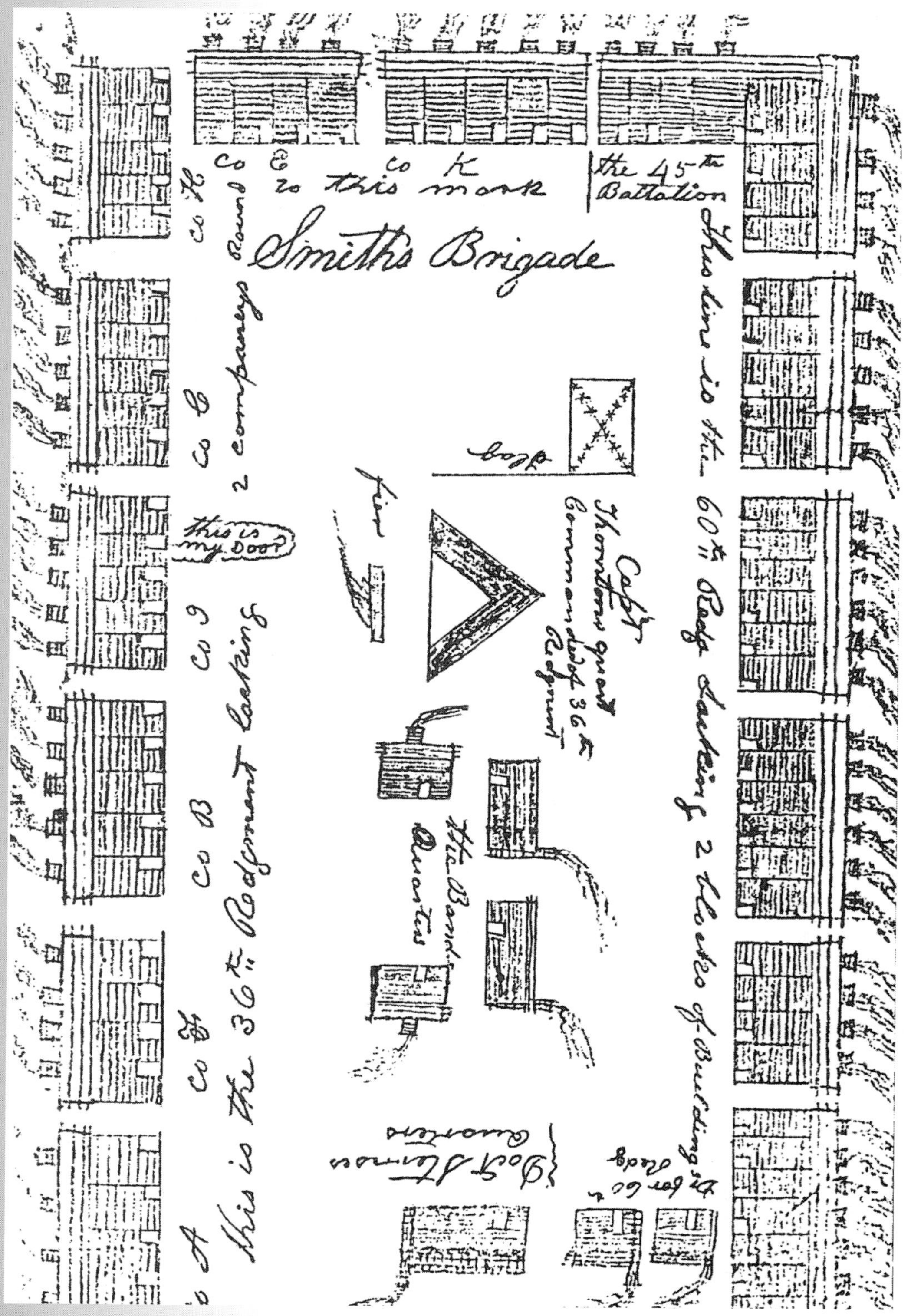
Co E
Co K
to this mark
the 45th Battalion
Smith's Brigade
This line is the 60th Regt lacking 2 sheets of Building
Co H
Co C
Co G
Co B
Co F
this is my Door
This is the 36th Regiment lacking
Capt
Thorntons quart
box
fire
The Band
Quarters
Quarters

for Petersburg. By the end of the month, Evans', Grimes', Gordon's, and Pegram's Brigades would all follow suit in order to strengthen Gen. Robert E. Lee's army in the trenches at Petersburg. Echols' Brigade and King's Artillery Battalion would also leave Early's army, but unlike the others, they would go to southwest Virginia.

On December 19, Wharton's division arrived in Augusta County as the last of Early's infantry, and it went into winter quarters in the lowlands near Barren Ridge. The following day, unfortunately, much of Early's army mobilized again in response to Federal cavalry movements, and it marched in "severe sleet, hail and snow" before arriving outside Harrisonburg. As the Federal threat had since receded, the Confederates returned to Augusta County only to be called out once again in response to a Union threat in the direction of Charlottesville. Though they did not march this time, traveling in rickety wooden train cars across Rockfish Gap shielded the men very little from the elements. Again, the Federal threat was gone and, on Christmas Eve night, the Confederate infantry arrived at Fishersville and dismounted from the train cars.

On Christmas Day, Early's infantry was finally able to begin the construction of winter quarters. As the infantrymen struggled to make their winter homes, the artillerymen, already established in their village of winter huts, drew special rations that included sugar, coffee, and molasses, all rarities in the Confederate army.

Opposite page: Pvt. John P. Wilson of the 36th Virginia Infantry made this sketch of the winter quarters for Smith's Brigade near Fishersville.
FROM *60TH VIRGINIA INFANTRY*

Below: Wintry view from Barren Ridge, looking east toward Waynesboro.

From Barrenridge Road, turn right and proceed 5.6 miles. Merge right under the railroad overpass and then left on Greenville Avenue/ Johnson Street. Proceed .1 miles and turn right on S. New Street. Continue to E. Beverley Street and turn right. Gen. Jubal Early's part-time residence and headquarters during the winter of 1864–1865 is 50 yards on the right.

STOP NO. 63

GEN. EARLY'S STAUNTON HEADQUARTERS

Gen. Jubal Early's winter headquarters in Staunton.

Continue along E. Beverley Street for .1 miles to N. Coalter and turn right. Proceed approximately .1 miles and turn left on Frederick Street. Proceed .2 miles and turn left on S. Augusta Street. Continue toward the Staunton Depot. American Hotel is just to the right of the depot, on the left side of S. Augusta Street.

Establishing his headquarters here as early as December 22, Gen. Jubal Early became a temporary resident of Staunton over the winter of 1864–1865. On January 10, 1865, Early issued the following order shortly after his return from a visit with Gen. Robert E. Lee in Richmond: "Commissaries and quartermasters and their agents are forbidden from impressing any supplies purchased by agents for Augusta County for the families of soldiers. All commanding officers should see that this order is followed."

Despite the order, the *Staunton Vindicator* at once made an appeal to the citizens of Augusta to look after the welfare of the men, who were obviously in dire circumstances that winter. The article read as follows:

> This distinguished officer has so disposed his troops as to afford ample protection to the County of Augusta. Their continuance in their present position will depend on the spirit that may be manifested by the people. The Army must be fed. The people have the means of doing it. If they wish protection for their families and property, they must supply their defenders with the necessaries of life. If these cannot be furnished, the troops must be removed, and the country left open to the incursions of the enemy. An enlightened self-interest therefore, (to say nothing of patriotism) demands that the farmers should act with liberality. One fifth of their surplus will maintain the army. Common sense would dictate the propriety of even giving that much to save the residue. But this is not asked. All that is required is that they shall sell, at moderate prices, a small part of their crops, to ensure the safety of their families and firesides.

STOP NO. 41B

AMERICAN HOTEL/THE STAUNTON ARTILLERY BANQUET

From American Hotel, proceed .1 miles toward S. Lewis Street and turn right. Proceed .1 miles and turn right on W. Johnson Street. Proceed .2 miles to S. New Street and turn left. The Virginia Hotel was located where the parking garage now stands.

On Saturday, January 28, the Staunton Artillery assembled at the American Hotel to be treated to dinner. After an elaborate meal and speeches by both General Early and Col. William H. Harman, the men left with full stomachs and in high spirits. Not long after the dinner, the men assembled again in their camp near Fishersville and drafted a set of resolutions calling for diligence and dedication to the Cause:

> We are fighting for liberty! The despondency talke[d] of does not exist in the army. The same spirit animates us now which inspired

> us in 1861. We are determined to never acquiesce in any accommodation short of the independence of our Confederacy—we believe this to be the spirit of the whole army; and we appeal to the people of our loved homes to respond to it; especially we demand it of our Congress. . . .

Col. Wilfred E. Cutshaw.
FROM *LONG ARM OF LEE*

One of the resolutions cited specifically at the banquet, which "cheered" their hearts, was "We now renew our pledge, given nearly four years since, to defend their liberties and ours, to the bitter end."

The same day that the resolutions were published in the *Vindicator*, the men of the Staunton Artillery, along with the rest of Cutshaw's Battalion, boarded a train at the nearby depot bound for Petersburg. Braxton's Battalion would follow later in the month, leaving only William Nelson's Battalion in Augusta County as the last of the guns for Early's army.

SITE OF THE VIRGINIA HOTEL — STOP NO. 20B

On February 21, 1865, Capt. Jesse McNeill's band of Partisan Rangers and a handful of men from Company F, 7th Virginia Cavalry—approximately sixty men in all—conducted a daring raid to Cumberland, Maryland. After getting through Federal picket lines, and in the face of nearly 10,000 Union soldiers stationed around the western Maryland town, McNeill's men crept into Cumberland and captured Generals Benjamin F. Kelley and George Crook. That

Capture of Crook and Kelley.
FROM *THE LAUREL BRIGADE*

Right: Gen. Benjamin F. Kelley.
FROM *GENERALS IN BLUE*/
THE WARNER COLLECTION

Far Right: Gen. George Crook.
FROM *PHOTOGRAPHIC HISTORY OF THE CIVIL WAR*

evening, Kelley slept in the Barnum Hotel while Crook spent the night at the Revere House. The Revere House was a hotel owned by a Mr. Daily, whose daughter, Mary, later became Crook's wife. Perhaps one of the most interesting parts of this story is that one of Daily's sons was a member of McNeill's Rangers.

After a harrowing journey back through the picket lines, across the Potomac and back into Confederate lines, the handful of Confederates, no doubt, felt a great sense of accomplishment. Upon reaching Harrisonburg on February 24, the Union generals were loaded in an old stagecoach and sent to General Early's headquarters in Staunton. Later that evening, the two dined at the Virginia Hotel and spent time conversing with General Early. During Crook's brief stay in town, the citizens must have appreciated the irony that Crook had, only eight months before, been at the head of one of the armies that had occupied Staunton. The following day the generals were loaded onto a train bound for Richmond, where the two were taken to Libby Prison. They remained in Richmond until they were paroled and exchanged.

From the site of the Virginia Hotel, continue along New Street for .1 miles and turn left on Frederick Street. Continue .6 miles and turn right on W. Beverley Street. Proceed 9 miles and turn left on Rt. 703/Hewitt Road. Proceed 2.2 miles. Ruins of the postwar depot will be on the left.

STOP NO. 64A

SWOOPE'S DEPOT

While the artillery and infantry made their winter home near Fishersville, Early's cavalry, under Gen. Thomas L. Rosser, made winter quarters on the Harrison Teaford Farm, just south of this point and just to the north of Sugar Loaf Mountain. On December 16, the 11th Virginia Cavalry arrived from Timberville as the first elements of Rosser's cavalry. Two days later, Shoemaker's Horse Artillery joined the cavalry at Teaford's and began to construct winter quarters. However, as with the infantry, camp was broken in December when Rosser led his troopers against a feint led by Gen. George A. Custer. In a surprise attack, he threw back the Federals at Lacey Springs, in Rockingham County. As the Confederate cavalry made its way back toward Swoope's, again, a Federal threat necessitated redirection of cavalry toward Charlottesville. By December 24, much of the cavalry had returned to the Teaford Farm, where its members continued construction of winter quarters.

Unlike the infantry, however, the cavalry with its horses to maintain, required more supplies than what the land had to offer. As the winter progressed, it was frequently necessary to temporarily disband companies so that they could return to their homes and find provisions on their own for the winter. Some, however, were not as fortunate; their homes were now behind enemy lines. For them, Swoope would remain their home for a greater part of the winter.

Desperately in need of supplies, Rosser performed one of the greatest feats of daring that winter by attacking the Federal garrison at Beverly, in Randolph County. Despite horrible weather conditions and a treacherous journey of some 75 miles, Rosser's raiding party of 300 men, all volunteers, departed Swoope on January 7 and returned on January 18, bringing with them much needed clothing and supplies, and over 600 Union prisoners who endured a grueling foot march as prisoners. In Staunton, these Federals were soon loaded aboard trains bound for Prisoner of War Camps.

Continue along Rt. 703/Hewitt Road for .25 miles and turn right on Rt. 876/Cattleman Road. The entrance to Wheatlands is .75 miles on the left.

Map showing the route of Rosser's cavalry to and from the raid on Beverly, Virginia.
FROM *ATLAS TO ACCOMPANY THE OFFICIAL RECORDS OF THE UNION AND CONFEDERATE ARMIES*

Claiborne Mason House/"Wheatlands."

STOP NO. 65

CLAIBORNE R. MASON HOUSE/ "WHEATLANDS"

During the winter of 1864–1865, both Gen. Thomas L. Rosser and Gen. Fitzhugh Lee are believed to have stayed at this house at different times. However, because Lee was still recovering from a wound he had received at the Battle of Winchester, his stay here was very brief. With the transfer of Gen. Wade Hampton to South Carolina in January, Lee, a nephew to Gen. Robert E. Lee, was appointed chief of the cavalry of the Army of Northern Virginia. He would command the cavalry until the end at Appomattox.

Claiborne Rice Mason.
COURTESY OF THE MASON & HANGER-SILAS MASON COMPANY

"Wheatlands" was the home of Claiborne Rice Mason. Born about 1804 near Troy, New York, Mason was a successful construction engineer for several Virginia railroad lines before the Civil War. Moving to Staunton in 1855, Mason moved to this house a few years later. In 1861 his assets were estimated at one million dollars. Like Jedediah Hotchkiss, this New Yorker considered Virginia his home, and, in 1861, offered his services to the Confederacy. Serving first as a captain of Company H, 52nd Virginia Infantry, Mason was appointed quartermaster and transferred to the engineer corps.

Promoted to lieutenant colonel, Mason was appointed as engineer on the staff of Gen. Thomas J. "Stonewall" Jackson by the spring of 1862. Along with his corps of black pioneers, Mason was known to have performed miraculous feats in the construction of makeshift bridges during the 1862 Shenandoah Valley Campaign and during the Seven Days Battles around Richmond. Serving as quartermaster of the Augusta Guard in November 1863, Mason returned to his duties as engineer and was responsible for cutting roads for the Army of Northern Virginia during the Battles of the Wilderness and Spotsylvania Court House. He was later assigned as the engineer responsible for the repair of the Virginia Central Railroad in Augusta County from 1864 to 1865.

Gen. Fitzhugh Lee.
COURTESY OF THE LIBRARY OF CONGRESS

Though he lost his wealth as a result of the war, Mason rebuilt his company, helped to rebuild the Virginia Central Railroad after the war, and was involved with many other successful construction projects with railroads in Tennessee, Kentucky, Pennsylvania, and Ohio. Interestingly, Mason's brilliance as an engineer stood in stark contrast to the fact that he was illiterate and could only copy his name. He died in Swoope in 1885 and was buried in Thornrose Cemetery.

From "Wheatlands," continue along Rt. 876 for 2.4 miles and turn left on Rt. 708. Continue .9 miles. Walnut Grove will be on the left.

Jacob Baylor House/ "Walnut Grove"

Stop No. 18B

On December 31, 1864, after a few days' stay at "Rose Hall" in Waynesboro, General Rosser, his wife, and four-month-old baby daughter arrived at Swoope's Depot. Though Rosser may have accepted the hospitality of several homes during his time here, he probably made his headquarters at the Baylor home "Walnut Grove"; one officer recorded having found him there on January 5.

Within days of his arrival, Rosser, the former commander of the famed "Laurel Brigade," called for volunteers from each of his three brigades to go on the Beverly Raid. In response to his call, however, cavalrymen of Col. Munford's Brigade nearly mutinied. Capt. John Lamb of the 3rd Virginia Cavalry later recalled what transpired:

> On account of the worn down horses and dispirited men, an earnest protest was made. Col. Munford, Major Charles Old, and myself visited Gen. Rosser at his headquarters, asking that the raid be abandoned, or at least delayed.

Gen. Thomas L. Rosser.
FROM *PHOTOGRAPHIC HISTORY OF THE CIVIL WAR*

Rosser immediately denied their request and, on the following day, an exchange of dispatches between Rosser and Munford resulted in

Jacob Baylor House/"Walnut Grove."

From this site, continue 1.2 miles and turn left, remaining on Rt. 708. Proceed for 1.15 miles and turn right on Rt. 703/Hebron Road. Continue 1 mile and turn right on Rt. 693/Cedar Green Road. Continue 1.9 miles and turn left on Rt. 252 North/ Middlebrook Road. Merge right on Rt. 262 East and travel for 2.7 miles and stay left to take I-64 East/I-81 North. Continue for 1.6 miles and take Exit 221/I-64 East. Continue 4.2 miles and turn right to Exit 91. Turn left on Rt. 285/Tinkling Spring Road.

Rosser placing Munford under arrest and preferring charges against him for sedition and conspiracy. Upon Rosser's return from the raid, a court was convened and Munford was acquitted of all charges. However, the ill feelings between Rosser and the men of Munford's Brigade remained. When one trooper returned from horse furlough to Munford's camp, he found "the horses starving to death" and the men "on the eve of mutiny." "The men looking like graven images were crowded around sickly fires that we could scarcely keep burning the rain came down in such torrents."

Fortunately for Munford and his men, on January 11 they were ordered to Waynesboro and then across the Blue Ridge; eventually they were detached from Rosser's command.

Before departing this site, take a look to the south and you can see Sugar Loaf Mountain and the area leading toward it. The tattered remnants of Rosser's Cavalry occupied these fields during the winter of 1864–1865.

A glimpse of the winter terrain around Sugar Loaf Mountain. Many Confederate cavalrymen, whose homes remained behind enemy lines, spent a harsh winter here.

Tinkling Spring Presbyterian Church. The cemetery behind the church contains some interesting headstones for the many Confederate veterans buried here—some having served as ministers at this church after the war. Stonewall Jackson's chief of staff, Dr. Robert L. Dabney, preached here in the 1840s. (Site G)

From Tinkling Spring Church, continue 1.2 miles on Rt. 285 toward Fishersville. Turn right on Rt. 250 East. Proceed 4.7 miles. Somewhere along the north side of this street stood Bruce's Tavern.

Stop No. 66

Site of Bruce's Tavern

On December 27, 1864, Bruce's Tavern hosted Gen. Fitzhugh Lee. During his stay, the local band "gave him a daylight serenade. It was a sort of 'gala Day' for old Waynesboro."

Bruce's Tavern, Waynesboro.
From *Waynesboro Days of Yore*

Continue .1 miles on Main Street and turn left on Wayne Avenue. Proceed .1 miles and turn left on Broad Street. Proceed .1 miles and turn right at Willow Oak Plaza Shopping Center to the site of "Rose Hall" that stood near the center of where the shopping plaza stands today.

Stop No. 27c

Site of the Hugh Gallaher House/ "Rose Hall"

Throughout the war, many prominent Confederates frequented "Rose Hall," where the Gallaher family "entertained many distinguished officers of the Confederate army and soldiers sleeping on pallets often taxed the capacity of the rooms, attic, etc." While staying here briefly in December 1864, General Rosser was invited by Mrs. Gallaher to return to Hanover Court House and bring back his wife and baby daughter. They stayed here before heading on to the Baylor home near Swoope's Depot.

Right: Capt. Hugh McGuire.
From *The Laurel Brigade*

Far Right: Rev. William T. Richardson.
From *Centennial History of the First Presbyterian Church of Waynesboro, Va.*

On January 12, 1865, the home served as the setting for the marriage of Capt. Hugh McGuire (Hunter McGuire's brother) and Sallie Bowen Gallaher. Presiding over the wedding was Rev. W. T. Richardson, the same minister who had sent off the men of Waynesboro in 1861. By all accounts, the wedding was a grand affair. Among the many officers who attended as groomsmen were Dr. Hunter McGuire, Maj. Henry Kyd Douglas, D. C. Gallaher, Maj. Gen. Fitzhugh Lee, Capt. O. R. Funsten, Capt. William McDonald, and Gen. Lunsford Lomax.

Kyd Douglas, having just arrived from yet another wedding outside the Valley, recalled, "His bride was fair and worthy of him. My bridesmaid was, in beauty, compared to the bride, as a pink rose to a red. . . . It was a merry, merry wedding." The party and dancing that followed the 8 p.m. wedding lasted well into the night, concluding at about 2:30 a.m.

Sadly, the groom was among the last casualties of the Confederacy; he was killed at Amelia Springs on April 6, 1865. In their short time together, Sallie conceived a child, Mary Holmes McGuire, whom her father would never know.

13 Greenville: The Augusta Lee Rifles and Gen. Robert D. Lilley
14 Jacob Baylor House/"Walnut Grove"
15 Wilson House/"Idle Wilde": the 5th Va. Inf.
16 Jedediah Hotchkiss House/"Loch Willow"
17 St. James Church
18 James E. Hanger Marker
19 Rockfish Gap & the Virginia Central RR
21 West View
22 The Parkersburg Turnpike
23 Site of Mountain House
24 Fort Edward Johnson
25 Mt. Solon
28 Stonewall Jackson Prayer Oak
31 Elizabeth Grattan House/"Contentment"
32 Mt. Meridian
33 Crawford House/"Bonnie Doon"
34 Crawford Run
35 Confederate Defenses at Piedmont
36 Moor's Attack
37 Thoburn Attacks
38 Providence Methodist Church
39 The March to Staunton
42 Hebron Church
43 Waynesboro
44 Mt. Torry Furnace
46 James Bumgardner, Jr. House/"Bethel Green"
47 Middlebrook
48 John Sproul House/"Locust Grove"
49 The Samuel Cline House
50 Weyers Cave Action
54 Patrick Family House/"Locust Isle"
55 Hermitage/The Weade Family
56 David Coiner House/"Long Meadows"
57 Cornelius Shaver Farm
58 Thomas McCue House/"Belvidere"
59 Burke's Mill
60 Mossy Creek Iron Works
61 Mt. Sidney
62 Barrenridge/Infantry and Artillery Winter Quarters
64 Swoope's Depot
65 Claiborne R. Mason House/"Wheatlands"
67 Christians Creek
A Philip O. Palmer House/"Valley Mills"
B Augusta Military Academy
C Hanger's Tavern
D Cornelius Shaver House
E Beard Family House/"Belmont"
F Battle of Piedmont VCWT Marker
G Tinkling Spring Presbyterian Church

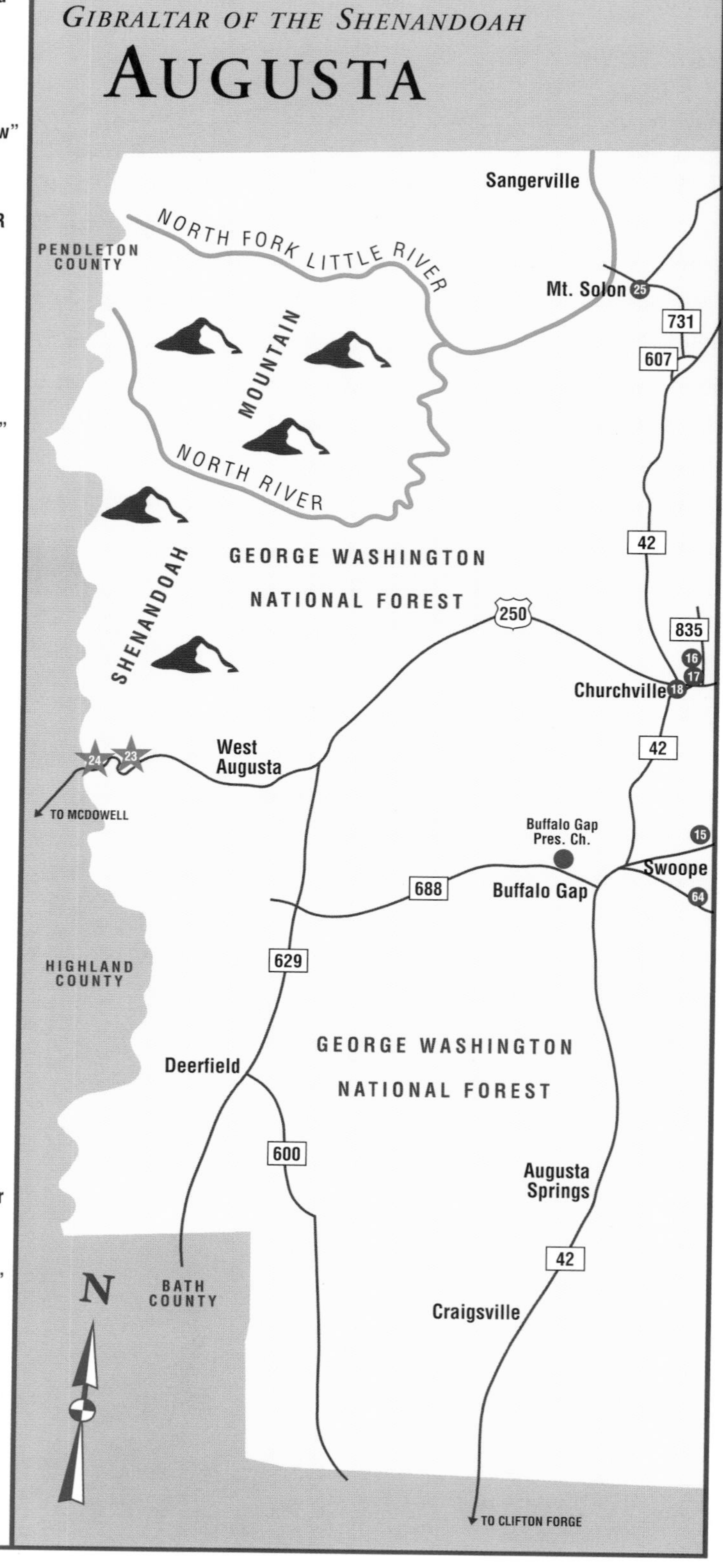

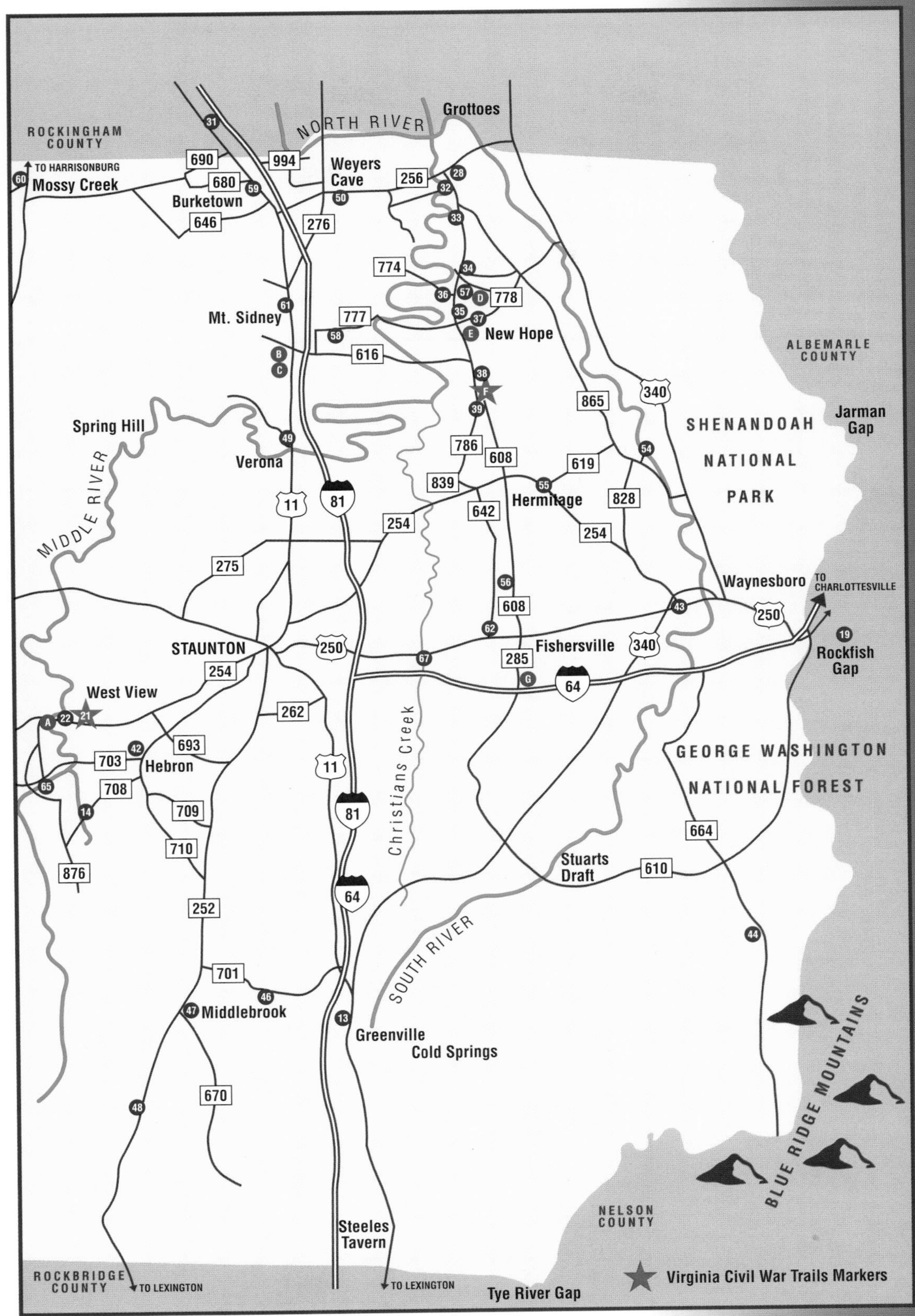
ROCKINGHAM COUNTY
TO HARRISONBURG
Mossy Creek
Burketown
Weyers Cave
Grottoes
NORTH RIVER
Mt. Sidney
New Hope
ALBEMARLE COUNTY
Spring Hill
Verona
MIDDLE RIVER
Hermitage
SHENANDOAH NATIONAL PARK
Jarman Gap
Waynesboro
TO CHARLOTTESVILLE
STAUNTON
Fishersville
Rockfish Gap
West View
Hebron
Christians Creek
GEORGE WASHINGTON NATIONAL FOREST
Stuarts Draft
SOUTH RIVER
Middlebrook
Greenville
Cold Springs
BLUE RIDGE MOUNTAINS
NELSON COUNTY
Steeles Tavern
ROCKBRIDGE COUNTY
TO LEXINGTON
TO LEXINGTON
Tye River Gap
Virginia Civil War Trails Markers

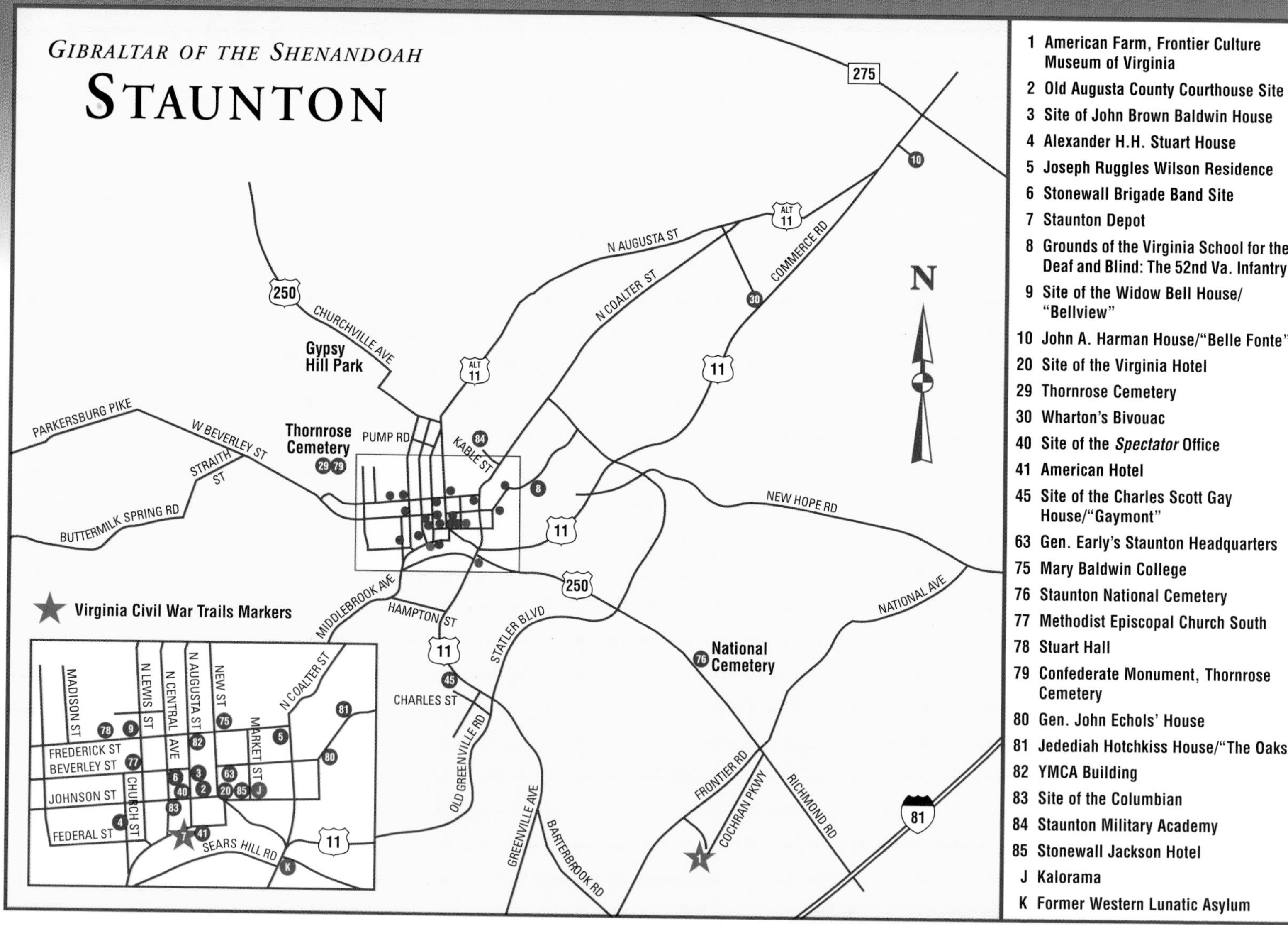
Gibraltar of the Shenandoah
Staunton
1 American Farm, Frontier Culture Museum of Virginia
2 Old Augusta County Courthouse Site
3 Site of John Brown Baldwin House
4 Alexander H.H. Stuart House
5 Joseph Ruggles Wilson Residence
6 Stonewall Brigade Band Site
7 Staunton Depot
8 Grounds of the Virginia School for the Deaf and Blind: The 52nd Va. Infantry
9 Site of the Widow Bell House/"Bellview"
10 John A. Harman House/"Belle Fonte"
20 Site of the Virginia Hotel
29 Thornrose Cemetery
30 Wharton's Bivouac
40 Site of the *Spectator* Office
41 American Hotel
45 Site of the Charles Scott Gay House/"Gaymont"
63 Gen. Early's Staunton Headquarters
75 Mary Baldwin College
76 Staunton National Cemetery
77 Methodist Episcopal Church South
78 Stuart Hall
79 Confederate Monument, Thornrose Cemetery
80 Gen. John Echols' House
81 Jedediah Hotchkiss House/"The Oaks"
82 YMCA Building
83 Site of the Columbian
84 Staunton Military Academy
85 Stonewall Jackson Hotel
J Kalorama
K Former Western Lunatic Asylum
N
275
N AUGUSTA ST
N COALTER ST
COMMERCE RD
CHURCHVILLE AVE
Gypsy Hill Park
Thornrose Cemetery
PUMP RD
KABLE ST
PARKERSBURG PIKE
W BEVERLEY ST
STRAITH ST
BUTTERMILK SPRING RD
NEW HOPE RD
NATIONAL AVE
MIDDLEBROOK AVE
HAMPTON ST
STATLER BLVD
National Cemetery
CHARLES ST
OLD GREENVILLE RD
GREENVILLE AVE
BARTERBROOK RD
FRONTIER RD
COCHRAN PKWY
RICHMOND RD
Virginia Civil War Trails Markers
MADISON ST
N LEWIS ST
N CENTRAL AVE
N AUGUSTA ST
NEW ST
MARKET ST
N COALTER ST
FREDERICK ST
BEVERLEY ST
JOHNSON ST
CHURCH ST
FEDERAL ST
SEARS HILL RD

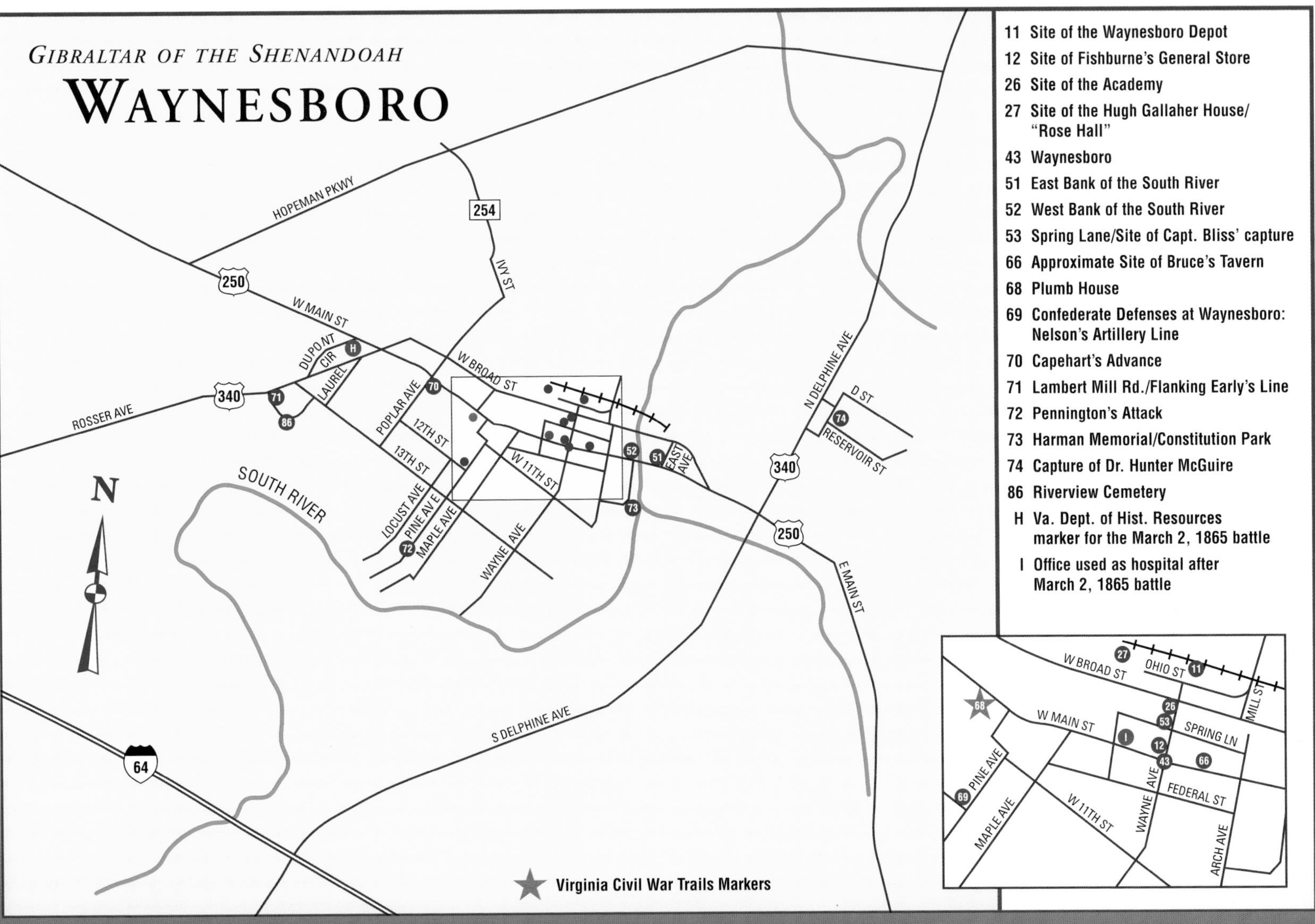
Gibraltar of the Shenandoah
Waynesboro
11 Site of the Waynesboro Depot
12 Site of Fishburne's General Store
26 Site of the Academy
27 Site of the Hugh Gallaher House/ "Rose Hall"
43 Waynesboro
51 East Bank of the South River
52 West Bank of the South River
53 Spring Lane/Site of Capt. Bliss' capture
66 Approximate Site of Bruce's Tavern
68 Plumb House
69 Confederate Defenses at Waynesboro: Nelson's Artillery Line
70 Capehart's Advance
71 Lambert Mill Rd./Flanking Early's Line
72 Pennington's Attack
73 Harman Memorial/Constitution Park
74 Capture of Dr. Hunter McGuire
86 Riverview Cemetery
H Va. Dept. of Hist. Resources marker for the March 2, 1865 battle
I Office used as hospital after March 2, 1865 battle
Virginia Civil War Trails Markers
N
HOPEMAN PKWY
254
IVY ST
250
W MAIN ST
W BROAD ST
DUPONT CIR
LAUREL
ROSSER AVE
340
POPLAR AVE
12TH ST
13TH ST
LOCUST AVE
PINE AVE E
MAPLE AVE
WAYNE AVE
W 11TH ST
EAST AVE
SOUTH RIVER
N DELPHINE AVE
D ST
RESERVOIR ST
E MAIN ST
S DELPHINE AVE
64
W BROAD ST
OHIO ST
MILL ST
W MAIN ST
SPRING LN
PINE AVE
MAPLE AVE
W 11TH ST
WAYNE AVE
FEDERAL ST
ARCH AVE

TOUR NO. 10 March 1865, The Final Curtain: The Battle of Waynesboro

Begin Tour No. 10 at the Samuel Cline House (Stop No. 49b) on Rt. 11 in Verona. Refer to the maps on pages 122–125 for assistance in locating the sites on this tour. This tour is approximately 39 miles in length and includes 12 stops at historic buildings and sites.

Stop No. 49b

The Samuel Cline House

From the corner of Rt. 11 and Bald Rock Road in Verona, proceed south for 3 miles to the fork and take the left fork in the road. Proceed for 6 miles (this road becomes Greenville Avenue/E. Johnson Street) and turn right on S. Augusta Street. Continue .1 miles and turn left on Frederick Street. Proceed for approximately .6 miles and turn right on W. Beverley Street. This road becomes Parkersburg Turnpike after leaving Staunton city limits. From the corner of Frederick and Beverley, proceed for approximately 9 miles and turn left on Rt. 703/Hewitt Road. Proceed 2.2 miles. Ruins of the postwar depot will be on the left.

After receiving orders from Gen. U. S. Grant, on February 27, 1865, Gen. Philip Sheridan launched on a campaign set on the destruction of the Virginia Central Railroad and the James River Canal, and, if possible, the capture of Lynchburg.

With 10,000 cavalrymen under Gen. Wesley Merritt, Sheridan's command pressed up the Shenandoah Valley toward Waynesboro. In addition to his many horsemen, Sheridan reported that "on wheels we had, to accompany this column, eight ambulances, sixteen ammunition wagons, a pontoon train for eight canvas boats, and a small supply train, with fifteen days' rations of coffee, sugar, and salt, it being intended to depend on the county for the meat and bread ration, the men carrying in their haversacks nearly enough to subsist them till out of the exhausted valley."

Early's ragtag command, by contrast, could not possibly stand up against such a large and well-supplied force. The command had already been severely depleted of men. Most had been transported into the trenches around Petersburg, some had been disbanded and sent home, and many had taken leave of the army for good. What was left of Early's army was barely surviving on meager rations. The end of the Confederate presence in the Shenandoah Valley was imminent, but Early scrambled nonetheless to bring together what he could to stand in Sheridan's way.

In the meantime, Staunton, with no real troops available for its defense, was being evacuated of all Confederate stores and supplies. Rosser, able to gather perhaps 150 men, moved ahead to North River to check the progress of the enemy as long as he could. The confrontation at Mt. Crawford, on March 1, could hardly have been called a skirmish.

Later that evening Merritt's cavalry went into bivouac here at Cline's Mill.

Swoope's Depot — Stop No. 64b

After his command arrived at Staunton, Sheridan learned that the Confederates had a substantial number of supplies out along the Virginia Central Railroad at Swoope's Depot. Early on the morning of March 2, a detachment of 300 men of the 20th Pennsylvania Cavalry, under the command of Maj. Robert W. Douglass, headed toward the depot.

Apparently, in advance of Douglass' detachment rode a band of fifteen Jesse Scouts (Federals clad in Confederate uniforms) who were bribed by a farmer in the vicinity to spare his barn, which contained a large amount of stores. Upon arriving at Swoope and learning of the activities of the Jesse Scouts, Douglass ascertained the men to be acting on their own, without authorization. Nevertheless, their deceit opened the way to many valuable stores that otherwise might not have been destroyed.

Ruins of the postwar railroad depot at Swoope.

Continue east along Rt. 703/Hewitt Road 4.5 miles and turn right on Rt. 693/Cedar Green Road. Proceed 1.8 miles and turn left on Rt. 252/Middlebrook Road. Proceed for 3.5 miles to S. Lewis Street and merge left .1 miles and turn right on W. Johnson Street. Proceed .1 miles and turn right on S. Augusta Street to reach the Staunton Depot.

Initially, the Federals found "immense quantities of commissary, quartermaster's, and ordnance stores." However, four local barns raised the most interest. These private barns contained some 3,000 pairs of boots, 3,000 blankets, 2,000 stockings, 2,000 trousers, 2,000 shirts and drawers, and 50,000 pounds of ham, shoulders, bacon, and beef, along with a small quantity of ordnance stores, consisting of small-arms and ammunition. Another rather detailed report revealed that 1,209 uniforms as well as a bridge over on the nearby railroad were destroyed.

Stop No. 7J

Staunton Depot

Following Sheridan's arrival in Staunton on the morning of March 2, destruction of Confederate buildings and stores was again in order, as it had been in June 1864. The 6th New York Cavalry, under Major Harrison White, was tasked with the job on this occasion. It went to work destroying all government property including the government blacksmith shop, a large tannery ("containing a large quantity of leather"), 17 stagecoaches, and 60 wagons.

While his men went to work burning, Sheridan considered his options. Should he go directly to Lynchburg or should he sweep east across Rockfish Gap toward Charlottesville? Since Early had left word that he planned to fight at Waynesboro, and, since Sheridan figured Early's troops to number no more than 2,000 men, he decided to move his forces toward Waynesboro and Rockfish Gap.

From the Staunton Depot, proceed to S. Lewis Street and turn right. Proceed for .1 miles and turn right on W. Johnson Street. Proceed .3 miles and merge right under the railroad overpass and turn left on Rt. 250 East/Richmond Road. Proceed 3.9 miles to east side of Christians Creek and pull off.

Stop No. 67

Christians Creek

On March 1, Col. Peter Stagg's Brigade of Gen. Thomas C. Devin's Division attempted to destroy the railroad bridge here, across Christians Creek. The attempt was started, but the heavy rains quickly extinguished the fires.

The following day, Sheridan, having occupied Staunton, ordered his cavalry forward to Waynesboro. In his memoirs he wrote that "the by-roads were miry beyond description, rain having fallen almost incessantly since we left Winchester, but notwithstanding the down-pour the column pushed on, men and horses growing almost unrecognizable from the mud covering them from head to foot."

As the Federals moved along Christians Creek, Rosser, with no more than 100 troopers, rode up and spied the bluecoat cavalry headed his way. According to D. C. Gallaher, "Rosser gave some orders to the

Far left: Col. Peter Stagg.
FROM *PHOTOGRAPHIC HISTORY OF THE CIVIL WAR*

Left: Dewitt C. Gallaher, son of Hugh Gallaher, owner of "Rose Hall" in Waynesboro.
COURTESY OF THE UNIVERSITY OF VIRGINIA

officer in charge of the small cavalry force with him and taking about half dozen of us with him he rode into the woods in bridle path until we reached a country road and then rode to Greenville and Staunton Road about 10 miles away. Rosser's object was to see for himself whether the enemy was going towards Lexington and Lynchburg or not, as General Hunter had gone nearly a year before. Then we rode on to the Middlebrook and Staunton road and there found no sign of the enemy." Rosser's idea was that the movement toward Waynesboro was a mere feint to cover his real movement to Lexington. But he was mistaken.

Continue east on Rt. 250 for 6.5 miles and turn left on Broad Street in Waynesboro. Proceed .5 miles and turn left into the Willow Oak Plaza Shopping Center. The site of Rose Hall is approximately in the center of where the shopping plaza stands today.

Rosser dispatched Gallaher to General Early to tell him that "none of the enemy has gone this way." "Off I rode in the rain" wrote Gallaher, "not knowing: where l would finally land, in Waynesboro, in prison or in another world." Ultimately, Gallaher would survive, but he would not be able to reach Early in time to make Rosser's report.

An early view of the Richmond Road looking west from Waynesboro toward Fishersville.
FROM *WAYNESBORO DAYS OF YORE*

Stop No. 27D

Site of the Hugh Gallaher House/"Rose Hall"

From the shopping center, turn right and proceed .1 miles on Broad Street. Turn left on New Hope Road and proceed for .1 miles. The Plumb House is immediately across the street.

On March 1, General Jubal Early made temporary headquarters here. Ordering Gen. Gabriel Wharton's two brigades and Col. William Nelson's artillery battalion from Fishersville to Waynesboro, Early hoped to set up his defenses on a ridge covering the approach to Waynesboro. He hoped to offer resistance for at least a day before withdrawing into Rockfish Gap. However, with as few as a thousand muskets and eleven cannons on the battle line, Early faced the worst odds he had seen since he had assumed command in the Valley. The ground on which he chose to fight, according to many present at the time, was poorly selected and spelled certain doom.

Early the next morning, Wharton's and Nelson's commands arrived from Fishersville and began to form on the ridge. While the troops moved in, Early and his staff took breakfast at "Rose Hall," where, according to D. C. Gallaher, Early turned down "a tumbler half full of whiskey." Gallaher continued that "it was a rainy blue morning in every way. My Mother sent the slaves, horses, wagons, etc., by my brother William across the Blue Ridge for safety. Everybody who had slaves, horses, etc., did likewise."

Stop No. 68

Plumb House

From the corner of New Hope and Main Street, turn left on Main Street and, after .03 miles, turn right on Locust Avenue. Merge to the left onto Pine Avenue and continue .2 miles and turn right on 12th Street. The parking lot on the immediate right is in the middle of the artillery position for Early's artillery during the Battle of Waynesboro.

Built between 1810 and 1820, the Plumb House is one of the few remaining original houses situated in the middle of the area that was the battlefield of March 2, 1865. At the time of the battle, Alfred and Mary Plumb lived here. As the Battle of Waynesboro swirled around this house, the Plumb family took refuge in the cellar. The family had already lost a son, Henry, who had enlisted early in the war in Company H, 5th Virginia Infantry, and was mortally wounded at the First Battle of Manassas. During the Battle of Waynesboro a Union cannonball struck the house and entered above the fireplace, going into the wall above the door opposite the fireplace, and cracking the door of the east room. The shot also shattered a mirror hanging above the mantel. Following the battle, Union soldiers who realized the obvious value of the pieces for use as field mirrors, took them from the house. Soldiers also took liberties in relieving the family of some food items as well. An ash cake baked by Mary Plumb before the battle was taken out of the skillet in the kitchen. In return, the soldier left some flour.

Circa 1890 view of the Plumb House.
FROM *WAYNESBORO DAYS OF YORE*

The house is currently being preserved under the auspices of the town and is the focal point for the interpretation of the Battle of Waynesboro.

Modern view of the Plumb House.

Stop No. 69

Confederate Defenses at Waynesboro: Nelson's Artillery Line

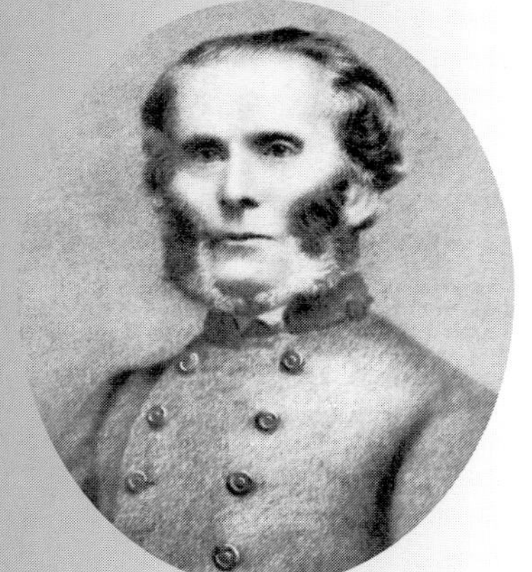

Col. William Nelson.
From *Long Arm of Lee*

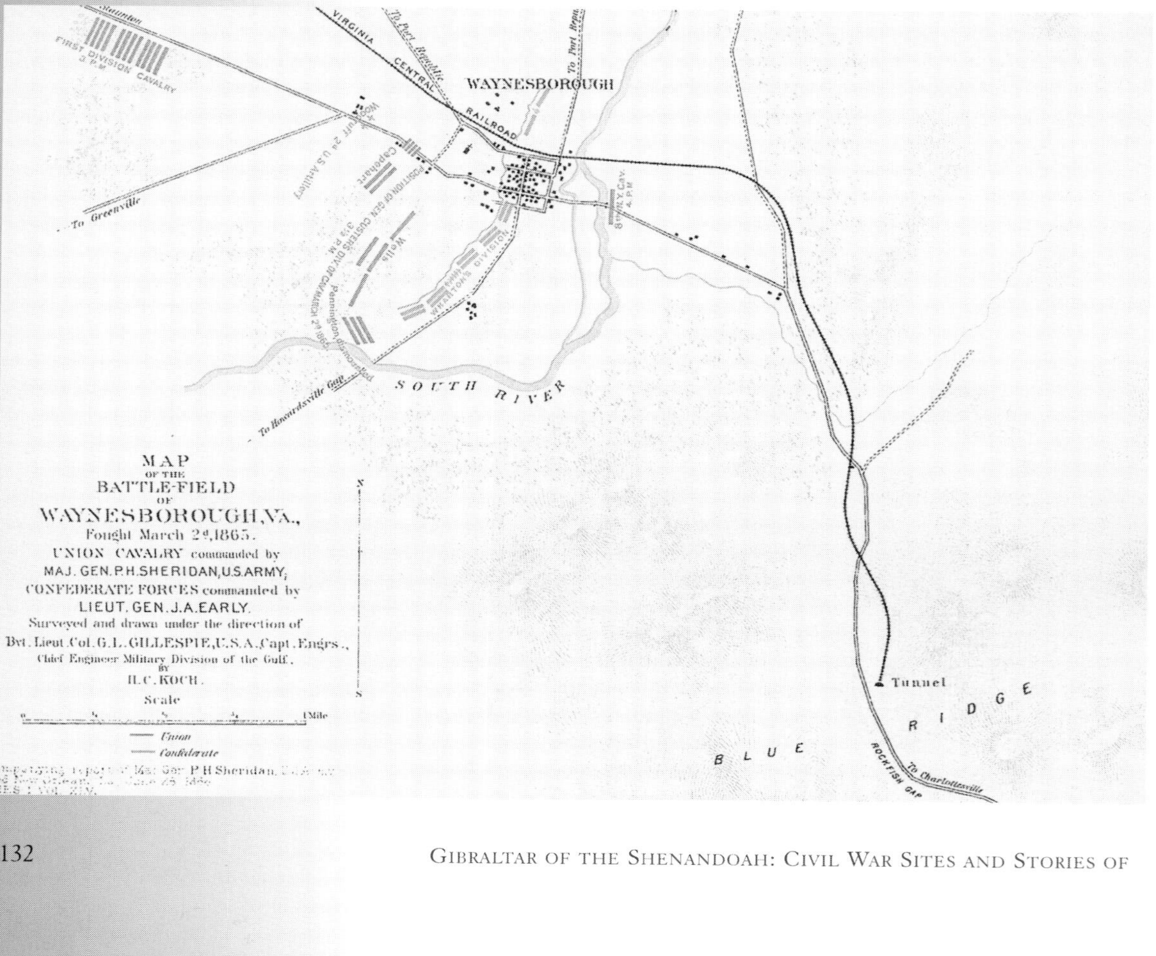

This position marks the center of the Confederate line, where most of the Confederate artillery was concentrated on March 2. The site overlooks the area of the initial approach of Custer's cavalry.

Jedediah Hotchkiss described the Confederate line that stretched to the right and left of this position: "The left at the edge of the woods northwest of town, and the right at the barn back of Gallaher's, with two pieces of artillery on the right, one just in rear and near the railroad and one more to the right on the river road." Wharton protested the placement of his men on this ridge and recalled later that his thin line was stretched for more than a half a mile and was "without breastworks or any protection except a few fence rails."

The poor position of this line offered no good. It backed up on the swollen river with only two bridges nearby. One bridge was on the east end of town and the other was a railroad bridge with planks laid across offering a narrow walkway. Wharton argued that the

Map of the Battle of Waynesboro, Virginia, March 2, 1865.
From *Atlas to Accompany the Official Records of the Union and Confederate Armies*

WAYNESBOROUGH
VIRGINIA CENTRAL RAILROAD
FIRST DIVISION CAVALRY
To Greenville
SOUTH RIVER
Tunnel
BLUE RIDGE
ROCKFISH GAP
To Charlottesville
MAP
OF THE
BATTLE-FIELD
OF
WAYNESBOROUGH, VA.,
Fought March 2d, 1865.
UNION CAVALRY commanded by
MAJ. GEN. P.H. SHERIDAN, U.S. ARMY;
CONFEDERATE FORCES commanded by
LIEUT. GEN. J.A. EARLY.
Surveyed and drawn under the direction of
Bvt. Lieut. Col. G.L. GILLESPIE, U.S.A. Capt. Engrs.,
Chief Engineer Military Division of the Gulf.
BY
H.C. KOCH.
Scale
1 Mile
Union
Confederate

defense should be taken across the river, to a defensive position on the south bank where gun pits already existed. Early, however, not believing that the Federals would attack, and certainly underestimating the numbers that he faced, refused to yield. In some ways, the situation at Waynesboro had a number of striking similarities to that which had existed just up the road at Piedmont, less than a year before.

Continue west on 12th Street for .2 miles and turn onto Poplar. Proceed .2 miles to the high school at the corner of Main and Poplar.

Capehart's Advance

Stop No. 70

When Custer's men reached a point near here around noon on March 2, they were greeted by Confederate artillery fire that briefly stalled their advance. Horace K. Ide of the 1st Vermont Cavalry recalled that "we could see infantry behind breastworks of rails, also some cavalry and the artillery spoke for itself; for as we formed in column of battalions they opened upon us, and as they knew the ground perfectly and appeared to have good gunners, they made it hot for us." In short order, Custer deployed Col. William Wells forward with the Second Brigade to probe Early's line. After a sharp exchange of fire, Custer decided against a frontal assault that could prove costly and he ordered a more careful reconnaissance in order to discern a weakness in Early's line.

When Custer determined that a gap lay between the Confederate left and the South River, he ordered Col. Alexander C. M. Pennington to dismount three of the regiments from the First Brigade and move to the right under cover of the woods. Meanwhile, Wells' men, supported by a battery of horse artillery, kept the Confederates occupied to the front. Col. Henry Capehart's Brigade, meanwhile, was ordered to prepare for a charge.

From the corner of Main and Poplar, turn left and proceed .28 miles to the corner of Main and DuPont. A state historical marker addresses the battle. Furthermore, from this point, look just to the northeast approximately 100 yards. This was the site of the Union horse artillery during the battle.

Far left: Col. Henry Capehart.
FROM *PHOTOGRAPHIC HISTORY OF THE CIVIL WAR*

Left: Postwar photo of Horace K. Ide, formerly of the 1st Vermont Cavalry.
COURTESY OF THE UNITED STATES ARMY MILITARY HISTORY INSTITUTE

Historical marker for the 1865 Battle of Waynesboro (Site H)

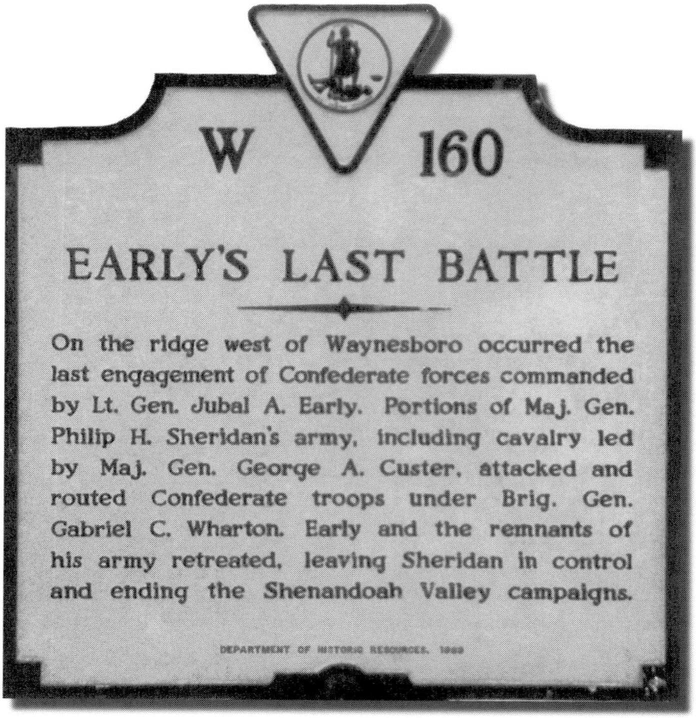

W 160
EARLY'S LAST BATTLE
On the ridge west of Waynesboro occurred the last engagement of Confederate forces commanded by Lt. Gen. Jubal A. Early. Portions of Maj. Gen. Philip H. Sheridan's army, including cavalry led by Maj. Gen. George A. Custer, attacked and routed Confederate troops under Brig. Gen. Gabriel C. Wharton. Early and the remnants of his army retreated, leaving Sheridan in control and ending the Shenandoah Valley campaigns.

From this corner, turn around and turn right onto Main. Proceed .1 miles and turn right on Rosser Avenue. Proceed .3 miles and turn left into the entrance of the Riverview Cemetery.

Stop No. 71

Lambert's Mill Road/ Flanking Early's Line

Continue straight .1 miles and turn left to exit the cemetery. Turn right on 13th Street and proceed for .5 miles. Turn right on Pine Avenue and proceed for .2 miles and turn right on 15th Street and pull over at the corner.

This road runs almost exactly along the old grade of the Lambert's Mill Road that was used by the Federal cavalry to flank Early's left.

Stop No. 72

Pennington's Attack

Near the end of the hour that it took for Pennington to reach the Confederate left flank, Early recognized the flanking maneuver and immediately sent orders directing Wharton to prepare for the attack. The dispatch was never received by Wharton and, by 3 p.m., the Federal flank attack was under way.

Armed with Spencer repeating rifles, Pennington's men quickly advanced on the Confederate line. At the same time, Capehart, with support from Federal horse artillery, charged headlong into the

Confederate center. According to Frederic Denison of the 1st Rhode Island Cavalry, "The Eighth New York and First Connecticut Cavalry, in columns of four, charged clean over the rebel breastworks, and then continued the pursuit of the enemy through the town, sabring the foe as they went."

Col. Ludwig August Forsberg.
FROM *FOREIGNERS IN THE CONFEDERACY*

The Confederates fired what was referred to as a "single ragged volley" and quickly began a general rout through town toward the bridges that were certainly not capable of handling the retreat of about 2,000 men. Also, having moved rapidly through the town and across the river, the 8th New York soon blocked the Confederate retreat from across the east bank of the South River. Swedish-born Col. Ludwig August Forsberg, commanding one of the Confederate brigades, later wrote that "many a veteran who had been with me for years and never shirked duty or refused to fight, now, discouraged and disgusted, hardly cared to fire his gun but doggedly threw down his arms and marched to the rear as a prisoner of war."

Hotchkiss, another witness to the rout, wrote that the scene was "one of the most terrible panics and stampedes I have ever seen."

The home and office of a local doctor during the war, this house was struck by a cannonball during the Battle of Waynesboro, sustaining little damage. It served as a hospital after the battle. (Site I)

Continue straight to Locust Avenue and turn right. Proceed .3 miles to the corner of 12th and Locust. Turn right on 12th and proceed to Pine Avenue and turn left. Proceed .1 miles and turn right on 11th Street and proceed .2 miles and turn left on Wayne Avenue. Proceed .1 miles and turn right on Main. Colonel Harman was killed in this general area, near Arch and Main Street, at the close of the battle. Continue .2 miles to McElroy Street and turn right into Constitution Park. The Harman Monument is in the far right corner of the park, near the river.

Stop No. 73

Harman Memorial/ Constitution Park

Originally placed near the site of Col. William H. Harman's death, this monument was moved several times before being placed at its present location.

As the Confederates found themselves surrounded, a trooper of the 1st Rhode Island Cavalry recalled, "Who can forget such sabers and spurs! Finding themselves rolled back and surrounded, the rebels threw down their arms and surrendered, and even cheered, as brave spirits might, for the bold and brilliant stroke by which they had been captured."

Throughout the town, Confederates who were able to do so took refuge in the houses of the village while others fought in vain against overwhelming Federal horse soldiers. Not far from this point, Col. William H. Harman was attacked by five men at the foot of Main Street hill, and was killed holding his ground to the last. A native of Waynesboro, Harman lived in Staunton and served as commonwealth's attorney of Augusta County from 1851 to 1863. At the time of his death he was also the grand master of Masons in Virginia.

Close-up of the Harman Memorial. Harman was buried in Thornrose Cemetery in Staunton.

WILLIAM H.HARMAN
Colonel. C.S.A.
Born Feb.17.1828
Killed in action at
Waynesboro Mar.2.1865.
He was lieutenant of a company from Augusta County in the Mexican War; afterwards Brig-General in the Virginia Militia; appointed Lieut Col.5th Virginia Inft. C.S.A. May 7.1861; Col. and A.D.C on staff of Maj. General Edward Johnson. May 17. 1862.
A Gallant Soldier.

Though he attempted to rally his men, Early realized the effort was useless. "I rode aside into the woods," wrote Early, "and in that way escaped capture. I went to the top of a hill to reconnoiter, and had the mortification of seeing the greater part of my command being carried off as prisoners." Early and over a dozen of his staff members soon after made their way from the scene and across the mountain.

Incredibly, the rapid onslaught of the Federal cavalrymen produced few casualties in the battle. A number of soldiers lay on the field dead and wounded, but an estimated 1,600 men, the majority, were taken as prisoners. Sheridan's horsemen captured 11 guns, 200 wagons, and 17 battle flags. Thirteen Medals of Honor were awarded for the capture of 14 Confederate flags, while two were awarded for the recapture of two Federal flags, including that of General Crook's headquarters. Though several Federal cavalry units were engaged in the fight, those at the front of the fight received the greatest number of medals awarded. Eight medals went to members of the 8th New York Cavalry (three from Company G alone), four to men of the 22nd New York Cavalry, and three to men of the 1st New York (Lincoln) Cavalry. One of the awardees from the 1st New York, Charles W. Anderson (aka George Pforr), later resided in Augusta County and died there in 1916. He is buried in Thornrose Cemetery.

Return along McElroy back to Main Street and turn right. Proceed across the South River for .5 miles and turn left on Rt. 340 North. Continue .4 miles and turn right on 5th Street. Dr. Hunter McGuire was captured near where the old Brandon Hotel was built years after the war.

Capture of Dr. Hunter McGuire — Stop No. 74

Attempting to escape capture, Dr. Hunter McGuire "reached a piece of woods" near this site. With pursuers close on his heels, McGuire attempted to jump his horse over a low rail fence and get into the woods. "But alas!," remembered D. C. Gallaher, "His horse fell with him!" Gallaher also recalled that "an officer told the fellow to put his gun down, saying, 'He's MY prisoner.'" When McGuire gave a Masonic sign of distress, a Federal officer, who was also a Freemason, saved the doctor's life. Taken to "Rose Hall," McGuire was treated well. He ate dinner that evening at the Gallaher home in the company of his "protector." Gallaher recalled that "the Yankee officer noticed a Knight Templar picture on the wall. It had my father's name on it. He inquired who this Hugh L. Gallaher was. When told he said, of course, he would protect his family and did. He also stopped their plundering and burning down at the Tanyard nearby."

Dr. Hunter McGuire.
COURTESY OF THE LIBRARY OF CONGRESS

The Confederate defeat at Waynesboro marked the end of large-scale fighting in the Shenandoah Valley, and the beginning of the last days of the Confederacy east of the Blue Ridge. Triumphant over his seven months of success in the Shenandoah Valley, Sheridan marched eastward and linked up with Grant in time to participate in a handful of engagements including those at Dinwiddie Court House and Five Forks. Custer, brevetted to brigadier general for his actions after Waynesboro, received the Confederate flag of truce at Appomattox. The surrender of Gen. Robert E. Lee's Army of Northern Virginia followed on April 9, 1865.

TOUR NO. 11 1865–1930, VETERANS, MONUMENTS, AND REMEMBRANCE

BEGIN TOUR NO. 11 AT MARY BALDWIN College (Stop No. 75) in Staunton. Refer to the maps on pages 122–125 for assistance in locating the sites on this tour. This tour is approximately 18 miles in length and includes 12 stops at historic buildings and sites.

STOP NO. 75 MARY BALDWIN COLLEGE AND POSTWAR OCCUPATION

Only months after Lee's surrender, Staunton's railroads had been repaired and postal service was restored. General John Echols traveled to Baltimore seeking capital to start a new bank to replace the banks that had failed during the war. Staunton's private schools resumed operations. The deaf and blind students returned to their facility and the Virginia Female Institute started up sessions once again. The Augusta Female Seminary, which had barely remained open during the war, was about to embark upon a period of unprecedented growth under the direction of a former student. When Mary Julia Baldwin

Early twentieth-century view of Mary Baldwin College, known at the time of the war as Augusta Female Seminary.
FROM THE HAMRICK COLLECTION

Modern view of Mary Baldwin College.

was engaged as the seminary's principal in 1863, no one could have foreseen the devotion with which she would pursue her task.

In November of 1865, civil authority was nominally restored and representatives were elected to the state legislature. The last Federal troops left Staunton on January 12, 1866, and Joseph A. Waddell wrote in his diary: "They were accused of exciting much disorder in the town and their departure caused general rejoicing in the community."

Gen. Isaac H. Duval, the first commander of the Federal troops that occupied Staunton until 1866.
FROM *GENERALS IN BLUE*/
WARNER COLLECTION

From Mary Baldwin College on the corner of N. New Street and E. Frederick Street, proceed along Frederick for .1 miles to N. Augusta Street and turn left. Proceed .1 miles and turn left on Johnson Street. Merge right under the railroad overpass and turn left on Rt. 250 East/Richmond Road. Proceed for 1.2 miles and turn around, taking Rt. 250 West to get back to the entrance of the National Cemetery on the right.

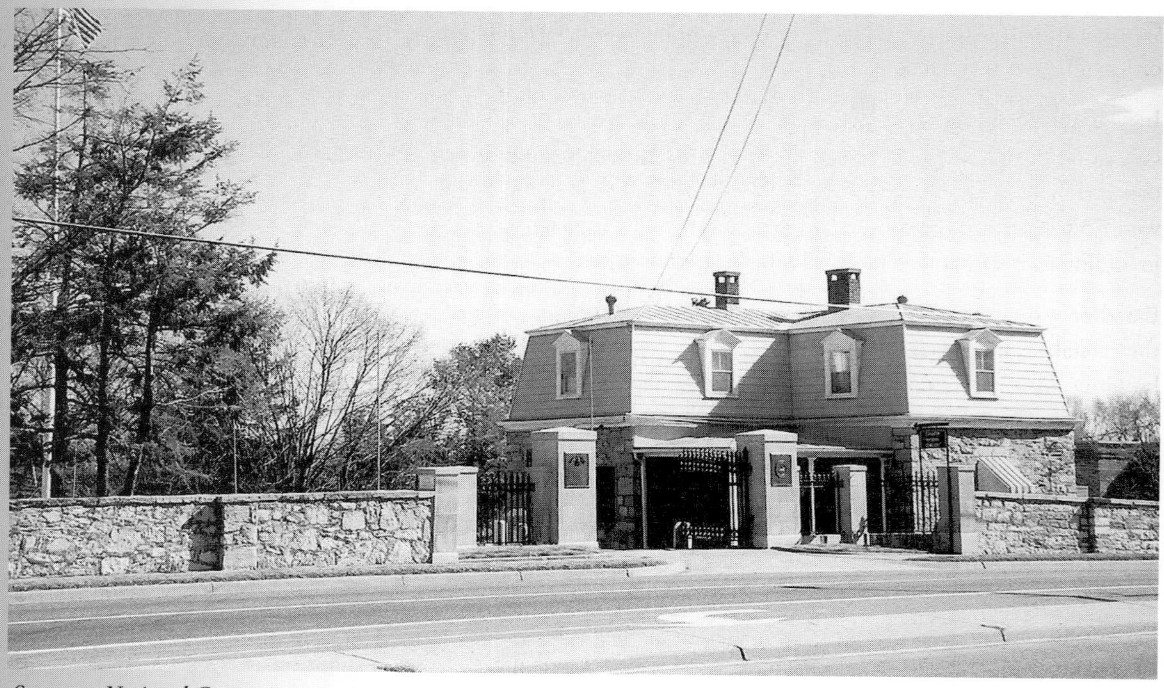

Staunton National Cemetery.

Stop No. 76

Staunton National Cemetery

Established in 1867, the Staunton National Cemetery or "Yankee Cemetery" as many local residents call it, became the final resting place for many Federal soldiers buried at several sites within approximately 100 miles. Many of the bodies were recovered from the nearby battlefields of Piedmont, Cross Keys, and Port Republic.

Sgt. Joseph S. Halstead, Company D, 12th West Virginia Infantry. Buried in Section B, Grave 402. Halstead, the color bearer for his regiment, was mortally wounded after crossing the Confederate works at the Battle of Piedmont on June 5, 1864.
Courtesy of the United States Army Military History Institute

Among the many fallen buried here is Capt. Nicolia Dunka, a Romanian-born soldier who cast his lot with the Union. Originally a member of the Hungarian Legion with Garibaldi in Italy in 1860, by the time of the Shenandoah Valley Campaign of 1862, Dunka was serving as aide-de-camp to Gen. John C. Fremont. In the action at Cross Keys on June 8, 1862, Dunka was carrying dispatches for Fremont when he was shot and killed by Pvt. John Long of Company B, 21st

Georgia Infantry. Papers found on Dunka's body included Fremont's order of march for that morning.

In the center of the cemetery, near the flagpole, is a monument consisting of an original cast-iron seacoast artillery tube secured by a concrete base. The inscription on the brass plaque states that there were 753 interments at the time of the placement of the monument, including 232 known and 521 unknown Union soldiers.

Based on a design by Quartermaster General Montgomery C. Meigs, the caretaker's lodge was not constructed until 1871. The brick utility building just outside the structure was built about 1887. Numerous additions and changes to the main structure were made at various times through the 1930s.

From the entrance of the National Cemetery, turn right on Rt. 250 East/Richmond Road. Proceed 1.1 miles and turn right under the railroad overpass and onto Coalter. Continue for .28 miles and turn left on E. Frederick Street. Proceed .35 miles. The parking lot next to the Central United Methodist Church marks the pull-off point.

Methodist Episcopal Church South — Stop No. 77

On the third anniversary of the death of Gen. Stonewall Jackson, Stauntonians began a tradition that would continue into the late 1930s. On May 10, 1866, a great number of local residents assembled at this church. Following memorial exercises, a procession, led by the Stonewall Brigade Band, marched to Thornrose Cemetery. In addition to addresses delivered by Col. Charles T. O'Ferrall, Capt. Jed Hotchkiss, and others, flowers were strewn on the graves of the war dead, while the band played various funeral dirges. An article in the *Staunton Spectator* later recalled that "attendance was large, a subject of 'grateful astonishment.'" Many misunderstood the activities; editorials in northern and western newspapers perceived the celebration as proof that the South was reluctant to display a truly repentant spirit.

From the parking lot, turn left and continue along Frederick for .05 miles. Stuart Hall will be on the right.

Col. Charles T. O'Ferrall.
From *Forty Years of Active Service*

Stop No. 78

235 W. Frederick Street

Stuart Hall

Established over twenty years before the Civil War as the Virginia Female Institute, the school was forced to abandon its buildings on July 21, 1861, to make room for use by the Institute for the Deaf, Dumb and Blind, whose own plant was needed as a Confederate military hospital. Though protests were lodged, the decision remained. After the end of the war, the trustees set about making repairs to return the school to operation. Eventually, in about 1880, Mrs. Flora Cooke Stuart, widow of Gen. J. E. B. Stuart, took over as director. Having moved to Staunton in the latter part of the 1870s, she was described as "a lady of rare attainments and peculiar qualifications for the position she is to fill. With all of the gentle qualities of a woman, who will care for the young girls under her charge as a mother, she is endowed with a clearness of judgment, a firmness of will and purpose, and a skill in administration which eminently fit her for the office she is to fulfill and for the efficient discharge of its high duties." Her charge of a mere $250 per session remained in place through 1898. Tuition included board, washing, fuel, gas, seat in church, calisthenics, and instruction in the English branches and Latin. Mrs. Stuart required a black uniform, not silk, for winter and white dresses or uniforms for spring. Mrs. Stuart banned all color from uniforms. She submitted her resignation in 1899 because of her sense of duty to her grandchildren. The name of the school was changed to Stuart Hall in 1907, in honor of Mrs. Stuart.

Continue along W. Frederick Street for .3 miles and turn right on W. Beverley Street. Proceed .1 miles to the entrance of Thornrose Cemetery on the right. After passing under the entrance arch, continue straight for .1 miles under the stone bridge, turn right, and continue .05 miles before turning left and continuing yet another .05 miles. The Confederate monument will be on your right.

Mrs. Flora Cooke Stuart,
widow of Confederate Cavalry legend,
Gen. J. E. B. Stuart.
From *Confederate Veteran Magazine*

Early twentieth-century view of Stuart Hall, formerly known as the Virginia Female Institute. The school originated as "Mrs. Sheffey's School" in her home at Kalorama (Site J).
FROM THE HAMRICK COLLECTION

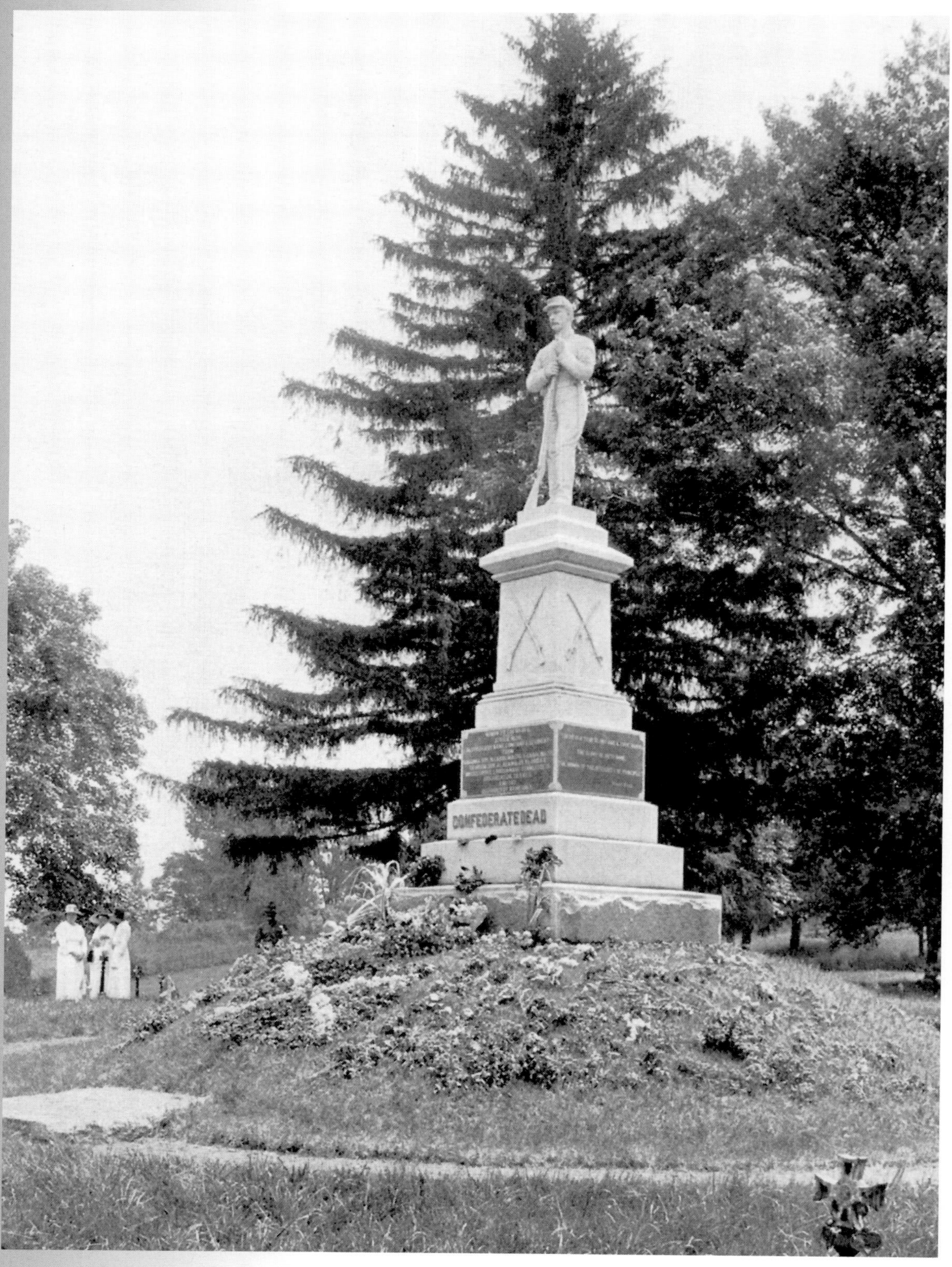
CONFEDERATE DEAD

Confederate Monument/ Thornrose Cemetery

Stop No. 79

As early as March 1866, several ladies of Staunton began volunteer work at Thornrose Cemetery, "determined they would fix up the graves of the soldiers buried at this place, and ornament the ground by planting suitable trees and shrubbery in it." In time that effort expanded to the May 10, 1866 celebration. By November of the same year, the Confederate dead buried on the battlefield at Piedmont and in the area near the winter quarters at Fishersville had begun to be gathered and reburied here. In time, these efforts evolved into what would become the Augusta Memorial Association, formed on June 18, 1870. With Col. James H. Skinner as president, the association was successful in enclosing the section with "handsome iron posts and chains and the marking of the graves with tags." On June 9, 1883, at the suggestion of Col. John D. Lilley, efforts were again expanded with the formation of a monument committee. Headed by Capt. J. N. McFarland, the committee was tasked with the "erection of a monument to the memory of the dead." A ladies' auxiliary was also formed under the leadership of Mrs. M. Erskine Miller. After the necessary funds were raised, the contract for the monument and statue was awarded to C. E. Ehmann, of Baltimore.

On Tuesday, September 25, 1888, the monument was officially dedicated with a huge ceremony. The procession that began from

Opposite: Circa 1919 view of the Confederate Monument at Thornrose Cemetery. A monument to the Augusta County war dead is located several yards behind the statue and at the end of the Confederate section.
From *Beautiful Thornrose: Memorial Edition*

Below: Modern view of the entrance to the Confederate section at Thornrose Cemetery.

A reunion of the Stonewall Jackson Camp, Confederate Veterans at Thornrose Cemetery in 1919.
FROM *BEAUTIFUL THORNROSE: MEMORIAL EDITION*

Staunton was composed of a number of organizations and was marshaled by Gen. Thomas L. Rosser, Capt. Thomas D. Ranson, and several others. Governor Fitzhugh Lee, Gen. Jubal Early, Maj. Jed Hotchkiss, and others rode in carriages along the route.

As a time-honored tradition since the 1880s, the ladies of the local J. E. B. Stuart Chapter of the United Daughters of the Confederacy, continue to hold, every Memorial Day weekend, an annual ceremony to honor the Confederate dead.

From Thornrose Cemetery, turn left on W. Beverley Street and proceed for approximately 1 mile (becomes E. Beverley Street). General Echols' house will be on the right at 324 E. Beverley Street.

Stop No. 80

Gen. John Echols' House

Continue on E. Beverley Street for .1 miles. Jedediah Hotchkiss House known as "The Oaks" is on the left at 437 E. Beverley Street.

Standing at 6′4″ and weighing 260 pounds, John Echols was a physically imposing man, but it was said that he rarely made an enemy and never lost a friend. A native of Lynchburg, Virginia, Echols was a graduate of Washington College and studied law at Harvard before being admitted to law practice in Rockbridge County in 1843. Before the war he served as commonwealth's attorney and as a member of the general assembly before representing Monroe County, Virginia, as a secession delegate. Echols initially voted against secession but voted for it in the second vote. A commander (as lieutenant colonel) of the 27th Virginia Infantry (part of the Stonewall Brigade), Echols was

Gen. John Echols' House. Jackson's engineer, Claiborne Mason, lived here in the mid-1850s.

wounded at the Battle of Kernstown in March 1862. After his recovery, he was promoted to brigadier general, and he served as commander of the Department of West Virginia until the spring of 1863. At the end of the war Echols accompanied Jefferson Davis to Augusta, Georgia. Resuming the practice of law after the war, Echols moved to Staunton, where he became a successful businessman. He also served as president of the Staunton National Valley Bank and helped to organize the Chesapeake and Ohio Railroad, ultimately serving as receiver and general manager. Echols also served as a Virginia legislator. In 1886, he moved to Louisville, Kentucky, but kept his ties with Staunton. He was one of the founding members of the Stonewall Jackson Camp of Confederate Veterans. He died in Staunton on May 24, 1896, while visiting his son, state Senator Edward Echols.

Gen. John Echols.
FROM *GENERALS IN GRAY*/
WARNER COLLECTION

JEDEDIAH HOTCHKISS HOUSE/ "THE OAKS"

STOP NO. 81

Though he had purchased the land years before, this last home of Jedediah Hotchkiss was not completed until 1888. While residing here, Hotchkiss spent much time writing about the war and working on the development of his mineral properties. Perhaps one of the great accomplishments during this time was his correspondence with British Col. G. F. R. Henderson, who was writing a biography of Stonewall Jackson. Henderson sent chapter proofs to Hotchkiss, which he combed through to ensure accuracy, even to the point of writing several of his old comrades. In this endeavor, Hotchkiss found himself at odds with the hyperbolic interpretations of former Jackson staff officer, Henry Kyd Douglas. Hotchkiss also spoke harshly against A. P. Hill. In partnership with Hunter McGuire, he also spoke out against Gen. James Longstreet's book that sharply criticized Gen. Stonewall Jackson.

Locally, he interacted frequently with Confederate comrades and he was among the original members of the Stonewall Jackson Camp. He became its commander in 1896, with F. B. Berkeley as adjutant. However, Hotchkiss' health failed him; on January 17, 1899, Hotchkiss joined many of the comrades who had preceded him. An article in *Confederate Veteran Magazine* noted that "the 'happy services' he always desired were simple, from his home, the Oaks. . . . The Stonewall Jackson Camp escorted him to his rest. . . . Over him were

Return along E. Beverley Street and turn right on N. Coalter Street. Proceed for .1 miles and turn left on E. Frederick Street. The YMCA is approximately .2 miles on the left.

"The Oaks," last home of Jackson's famous mapmaker Jedediah Hotchkiss.

placed three Confederate flags sent by tender hands. Of "the old staff" (Jackson's staff) Rev. James P. Smith, D.D., of Richmond, was the sole representative, who pronounced the benediction over the flower-covered grave of "one of the best of men."

Stop No. 82

YMCA Building

As early as May 7, 1889, a group of thirty to forty Confederate veterans had assembled at the Staunton City Council room and had proposed the formation of "The Augusta Association of Confederate Survivors." The purpose of the association was "simply social in character," but it had also been formed to counter those who "had been seen figuring at public celebration of Confederate soldiers, men who were not such, but were strutting in borrowed plumes." There was also a proposal to include sons of the Confederate survivors as members in the organization.

Meetings of the veterans continued over the next two years until, on Monday, June 20, 1892, the veterans formed another organization under an umbrella organization called the Grand Camp of Confederate Veterans of Virginia. Formed under the name of the

Stonewall Jackson Camp, it was soon chartered as Camp No. 25 of the Grand Camp of Confederate Veterans of Virginia, the fourth such camp to be chartered in the Shenandoah Valley.

As an extension of the veterans' organization, the J. E. B. Stuart Chapter, No. 156, and Waynesboro Chapter, No. 160, United Daughters of the Confederacy were chartered circa 1897. Mrs. J. E. B. Stuart, principal over the Virginia Female Institute, was the first president of the chapter named for her husband. The Stonewall Jackson Camp, No. 161, United Sons of Confederate Veterans, was chartered circa 1899.

The Stonewall Jackson Camp of Confederate Veterans was an extremely active camp. It was chartered yet again on March 20, 1894, as Camp No. 469 of the United Confederate Veterans.

Over the years, death took its toll on the membership. From 1910 to 1920 the camp lost over 134 members. Sometime after 1932, the camp was officially disbanded.

From the YMCA, continue .1 miles and turn left on N. Central Street. Proceed .1 miles to the corner of W. Johnson and N. Central. The Columbian was just across the street in front of you.

The YMCA in Staunton was originally organized by many Confederate veterans. The first YMCA building (now known as the Clock Tower) at the corner of Central and West Beverly Streets was the site of some of the earliest meetings of the Stonewall Jackson Camp. This second YMCA building, built in the early twentieth century, also served as a meeting site in the waning years of the organization.

The 1911 reunion of Confederate Veterans of the Stonewall Jackson Camp on Robert E. Lee's birthday.
FROM *BEAUTIFUL THORNROSE: MEMORIAL EDITION*

J. N. McFarland, fourth commander of the Stonewall Jackson Camp (1895–1896). McFarland was followed as commander by Hotchkiss and Opie. Note the specially made veteran's uniform and medal.
FROM *BEAUTIFUL THORNROSE: MEMORIAL EDITION*

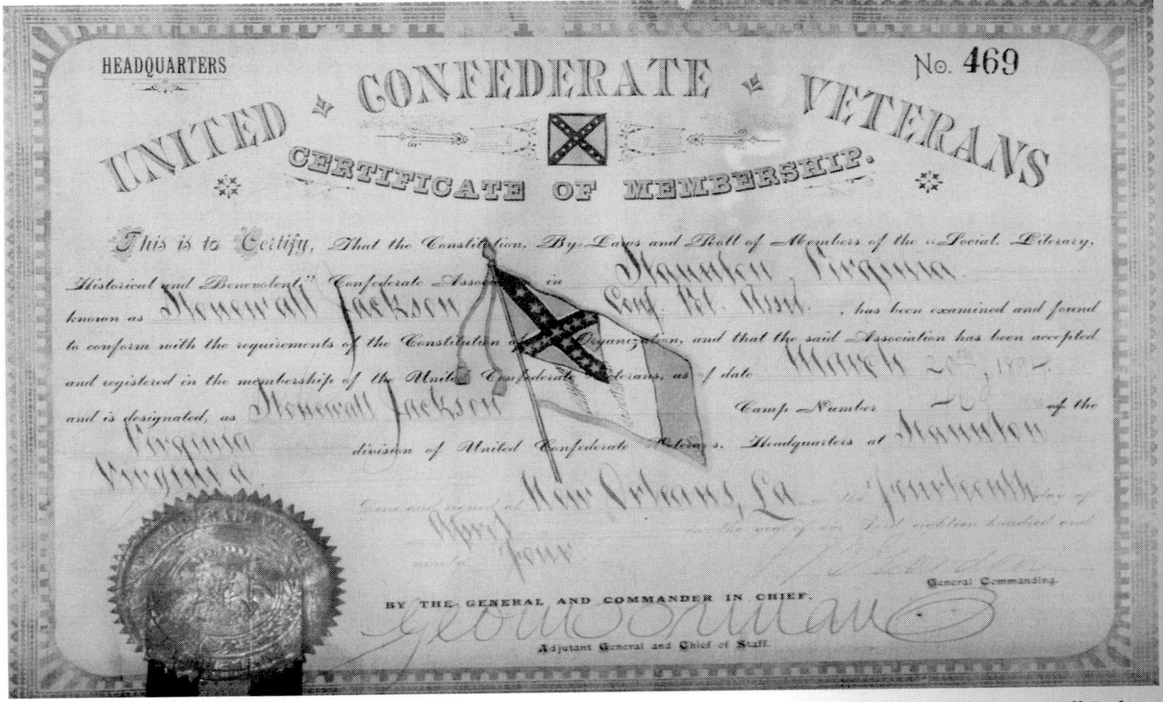

HEADQUARTERS

UNITED CONFEDERATE VETERANS

No. 469

CERTIFICATE OF MEMBERSHIP.

This is to Certify, That the Constitution, By-Laws and Roll of Members of the "Social, Literary, Historical and Benevolent" Confederate Association in Staunton Virginia known as Stonewall Jackson Conf. Vet. Assn., has been examined and found to conform with the requirements of the Constitution of this Organization, and that the said Association has been accepted and registered in the membership of the United Confederate Veterans, as of date March 20th, [illegible] and is designated, as Stonewall Jackson Camp Number [illegible] of the Virginia division of United Confederate Veterans, Headquarters at Staunton Virginia.

Done and signed at New Orleans, La. the fourteenth day of [illegible] in the year of our Lord eighteen hundred and ninety-four

General Commanding.

BY THE GENERAL AND COMMANDER IN CHIEF.

Adjutant General and Chief of Staff.

Above: Charter of the Stonewall Jackson Camp as a camp of the United Confederate Veterans.
Author's Collection

Left: Early reunion ribbon for the members of the Stonewall Jackson Camp. Note that this ribbon and the one worn by McFarland reflect "Camp 25," which was the number of the camp as it existed as a part of the Grand Camp of Confederate Veterans of Virginia organization. It was Camp No. 469 of the United Confederate Veterans.
Courtesy of John L. Heatwole

Stop No. 83 — Site of the Columbian Hall

At noon on Wednesday, October 10, 1900, strains of "Dixie" floated over the city of Staunton at the Columbian while the Stonewall Jackson Camp No. 25, Grand Camp Confederate Veterans, hosted thousands of Virginia Confederate Veterans at the opening of the thirteenth annual meeting of the Grand Camp of Confederate Veterans of Virginia. Running for three days, the meeting drew representatives from ninety-five camps that included an estimated 2,000 veterans.

Perhaps one of the largest draws for the convention was the "long talked of reunion of the Stonewall Brigade" which occurred at 3 p.m. on Thursday, October 11. This was followed an hour later by a reunion of the 1st Virginia Cavalry and an address by Gen. Fitzhugh Lee. Ultimately, the meeting served as the "seed" of future Stonewall Brigade reunions. Just over three years later, on October 22, 1903, the Brigade came together once again in Staunton and adopted a preamble and resolutions asking that "all Camps of Confederate Veterans and Sons of Confederate Veterans and Chapters of Daughters of the Confederacy be requested to observe the nineteenth day of January as 'Lee and Jackson Day,' that these heroes may be as united in the memory of their countrymen as they were in their service and their fame." Since the Commonwealth of Virginia still recognizes "Lee-Jackson Day" as a state holiday, it seems likely that the roots of the modern celebration came from that October 1903 meeting in Staunton, and the holiday may be rooted in the 1900 convention.

From the corner of Central and Johnson, turn left on W. Johnson and proceed for .3 miles and turn left on N. Coalter Street. Proceed for .4 miles and turn left on Kable Street. Proceed .1 miles and merge left. The Staunton Military Academy Mess Hall is less than .05 miles straight ahead.

Columbian Hall.
From the Hamrick Collection

Circa 1911 view of Staunton. Note Columbian Hall near the right center of the card. AUTHOR'S COLLECTION

STAUNTON MILITARY ACADEMY — STOP NO. 84

On June 17, 1925, the *Staunton News Leader* led off the day's paper with the announcement that "BUGLE BLAST WILL AROUSE VETERANS." For the first time since the reunion meeting of 1900, Staunton was again to play host to the ever-thinning ranks of the men in gray. Once again the Stonewall Jackson Camp No. 25 of Staunton hosted the opening of the thirty-eighth annual meeting of the Grand Camp of Confederate Veterans of Virginia, with 178 veterans staying in the barracks of the Staunton Military Academy. The convention opened at 10 a.m. on June 17. Housed in the barracks, eating their meals in the mess hall, and holding business sessions in the Academy's large gymnasium, in all, 468 veterans, or nearly one-third of the total membership of the Grand Camp Confederate Veterans of Virginia at the time, attended the convention, showing a stark contrast in numbers from 25 years before. "Not a single Confederate is allowed to walk in Staunton," noted the newspaper, as "dozens of automobiles bearing the invitation 'ride with me' were at the disposal of all wearers of the grey."

Commander H. M. McIllhany served as commander (1900–1901) of the Stonewall Jackson Camp during the first major Grand Camp of Confederate Veterans of Virginia reunion in Staunton.
FROM *STAUNTON: THE QUEEN CITY*

In addition to the meeting of the veterans, the Virginia Division, Sons of Confederate Veterans (renamed from United Sons of Confederate

Mess Hall at the Staunton Military Academy.
FROM THE HAMRICK COLLECTION

Veterans in 1912) convened their annual meeting with over 250 representatives from camps throughout the Commonwealth. While the Staunton S.C.V. Camp had been in existence since before 1899, by 1926, another organization, the Lee-Jackson Camp No. 410, was organized in Waynesboro. Though the exact date of its origins is unclear, both camps would eventually disband. A third camp would not emerge from Staunton until 1989 with the chartering of the John D. Imboden Camp No. 1504, which disbanded before 2000.

Having established the Charlestown Male Academy in Jefferson County, Virginia (now West Virginia) in 1860, William H. Kable moved the school in 1883 to Staunton. Like the Augusta Military Academy, Staunton Military Academy could also claim origins in a Confederate Veteran, for Kable had served as a captain and quartermaster of the 10th Virginia Cavalry from 1861. Like Charles S. Roller, Kable had also been present at the surrender at Appomattox Court House in April of 1865.

Reunion ribbon from the 1925 Virginia Division S.C.V. Convention in Staunton. AUTHOR'S COLLECTION

From the Staunton Military Academy parking lot, take Kable Street to N. Coalter Street and turn right. Continue .15 miles and turn right on E. Frederick Street. Proceed .1 miles and turn left on N. Market Street. Continue .1 miles to the Stonewall Jackson Hotel on the right at 28 South Market Street.

William H. Kable, founder and principal of Staunton Military Academy.
COURTESY OF THE STAUNTON MILITARY ACADEMY ALUMNI ASSOCIATION AND MUSEUM

STONEWALL JACKSON HOTEL — STOP NO. 85

Built in 1923, the Stonewall Jackson Hotel, the first fireproof building in Virginia, was once the "most modern hotel in the South." From September 30 to October 3, 1930, the hotel served as the site of the 35th Convention of the United Daughters of the Confederacy. Appropriately named for just such an occasion, it also held the irony of being the last building that would hold a major "Confederate" Convention in the city of Staunton which would also be host to the few remaining Confederate Veterans of the Stonewall Jackson Camp that remained in Staunton, Waynesboro, and Augusta County.

Stonewall Jackson Hotel.
FROM THE HAMRICK COLLECTION

A focus of the convention was the waning interest in the veteran celebration. Coupled with the ever-decreasing number of actual Confederate Veterans remaining, the effects of the Depression had a noticeable impact on the remembrance movement. "Business, depression and hard times have left their marks even upon the Virginia Division, United Daughters of the Confederacy," noted Mrs. Charles E. Bolling, state president. "It is with sincere regret that we record such a small increase in new members—a total of 357 in 1930 compared with 402 in 1929. There is cause for us to be greatly concerned over this situation for without life, which means growth, there must be stagnation."

From the Stonewall Jackson Hotel, continue straight to Kalorama Street. Turn right and proceed to Greenville Avenue and turn left. Proceed .1 miles and merge right under the railroad overpass and turn left on Rt. 250 East/Richmond Road. Proceed for 10.75 miles and turn right on Rosser Avenue. Proceed .3 miles and turn left on 13th Street. Proceed .1 miles and turn right into the Riverview Cemetery. The Confederate Monument is straight ahead in the circle.

Staunton's J. E. B. Stuart Chapter and all of Augusta County had seen an impressive record as a home for chapters of the United Daughters of the Confederacy (U.D.C.). Since the organization of the J. E. B. Stuart Chapter, in about 1897, under the care of Flora Cooke Stuart, J. E. B. Stuart's widow, the U.D.C. had grown tremendously in the county. The E. G. Fishburne Chapter in Waynesboro was organized not long after the Stuart Chapter, and then, by 1932, yet another, the C. R. Mason Chapter of Fishersville/Stuart's Draft, had been organized.

Stop No. 86

Riverview Cemetery/ 1906 Confederate Monument

Confederate Monument, Riverview Cemetery, Waynesboro.

On Thursday, May 24, 1906, a monument to the Confederate dead who are buried near Waynesboro, many of them unknown, was dedicated in Riverview Cemetery. Located in the circle within the cemetery, the monument bears the inscription "Our Confederate Dead" and "1861–1865." The names of Virginia veterans are on two sides while the fourth side bears the names of soldiers from Georgia (2), Louisiana (1), and Maryland (1).

Guests for the event began arriving in the early morning and they continued to arrive all day. According to the *Spectator*, "About four hundred went from Staunton, Stonewall Jackson Camp, Commander J. H. Waters in charge, took a goodly number." At 3 p.m. the procession formed on Wayne Avenue and marched out to Main Street to the cemetery, "headed by the famous Stonewall Brigade Band." Following behind the band were the cadets of the Fishburne Military School, the veterans, sons of veterans, Waynesboro Fire Department, carriages with speakers, floats with the young ladies who were a part of the afternoon ceremonies, and a mounted group of sons of veterans. After prayers and speeches, the monument was unveiled by

"Miss Ruth Bush, assisted by Misses Mary Ellison, Virginia Leftwich, Anne Shirkey, Kate Taylor, Jean Smith, Mary Peale, Alene Coyner, Catherine Holt, Agnes Stribling, Evelyn Culton, Emily Ellis, Mary Frances Bratton, and Nannie White, representing the states of the Confederacy. Following the unveiling, speeches were made by S. D. Timberlake Jr. of Staunton and Richard S. Parks of Luray. A benediction was then given by Rev. B. F. Ball of Mosby's Rangers and a salute given by the Cadet Corps of the Fishburne Military School."

Appendix A

Stonewall Jackson Camp Members as Transcribed from the July 1905 issues of the *Staunton News & Dispatch*

** This is not a complete list of all members as several applied for membership for years after 1905.*

Abney, William G., Brookewood, Va., Pvt., Co. L, 5th Va. Inf.

Alexander, S. H., Augusta Co., Va., Pvt., Co. E, 1st Va. Cav.

Alexander, S. T., Basic City, Va., Co. A, 36th Va. Inf.

Allen, Donald E., Kansas City, Mo., Pvt., VMI Corps of Cadets

Alman, James L., Staunton, Va., Pvt., Co. E, 28th Va. Inf.

Amiss, Sylvanus T., Staunton, Va., Pvt., Co. D, 4th Va. Cav.

Anderson, Andrew Perry, Staunton, Va., Pvt., Co. C, 14th Va. Cav.

Anderson, N. H., Staunton, Va., Pvt., McNeill's Rangers/courier for Gen R. E. Lee

Anderson, Robert J., Greenville, Va., Pvt., Co. E, 5th Va. Inf.

Anderson, William A. L., Staunton, Va., Pvt., Co. H, 14th Va. Cav.

Andrew, Nelson, Staunton, Va., Pvt., Co. I, 5th Va. Inf.

Argenbright, George W. C., Valley Mills, Va., Pvt. Marquis' Battery

Argenbright, Newton, Staunton, Va., Pvt., Col. Kenton Harper's Regt. Va. Inf., AACS Charter member

Armstrong, W. D., Staunton, Va., 1st Lt., Co. I, 18th Va. Cav.

Arnall, Charles Steele, Atlanta, Ga., Sgt./Adj. Co. L, 5th Va. Inf.

Ballew, James Lewis, Brookewood, Va., Pvt., Co. L, 5th Va. Inf.

Balthis, William L., Baltimore, Md., Capt., Staunton Artillery

Bartley, Vernon C., Greenville, Va., Pvt., Co. D, 5th Va. Inf.

Baxter, Jacob C., Mt. Solon, Va., Pvt., Co. F, 62nd Va. Inf.

Baylor, Charles W., Augusta Co., Va., Sgt., Co. D, 5th Va. Inf.

Baylor, G. M., Swoope, Va., Pvt., Co. A, Engineer Corps

Bear, Henry C., Lyndhurst, Va., Pvt., Co. A, 52nd Va. Inf.

Beard, John W., Moffat's Creek, Va., Pvt., Co. D, 5th Va. Inf.

Bell, Daniel McNeel, Staunton, Va., Sgt., Co. C, 5th Va. inf.

Bell, Franklin R., Ft. Defiance, Va., Pvt., Co. C, 5th Va. Inf.

Bell, H. M., Staunton, Va., Major, Quartermaster's Dept.

Belvin, Winchester Dunham, Parker's Battery, VMI & Co. B, 43rd Bttn. Va Cav.

Berkeley, Carter, Staunton, Va., Lt., McClanahan's Battery/AACS Charter member

Berkeley, F. B., Staunton, Va., Captain, and A.A. Gen., Gen. John D. Imboden's Brigade, AACS Charter member

Biby, Henry G., Augusta Co., Va., Pvt., Co. F, 52nd Va. Inf.

Bickle, Yeiser Morris, Staunton, Va., Pvt., Co. L, 5th Va. Inf.

Blackburn, James W., Sgt., McClanahan's Battery

Blackford, Benjamin, Staunton, Va., Surgeon, 11th Va. Inf. & Gen. Hospital (at Liberty, Culpeper and Front Royal, Va.)

Blackley, John B., Staunton, Va., Pvt., Davidson's Battery

Blakemore, John F., Stuart's Draft, Va., Pvt., Co. I, 5th Va. Inf.

Bledsoe, D. T., Abilene, Texas, 1st Sgt., Co. E, 25th Va. Inf.

Bolling, Stewart, Augusta Co., Va., Pvt., Wright's Battn. Inf.

Bosserman, James Christian, Pvt., Co. K, 5th Va. Inf.

Bradley, M. N., Staunton, Va., Pvt., Signal Corps

Brand, John W., Augusta Co., Va., Pvt., Co. E, 5th Va. Inf.

Brand, William F., Augusta Co., Va. Pvt., Co. E, 5th Va. Inf.

Britton, John Newton, Zack (and later Newport) , Va., Pvt., Co. C, 39th Bttn. Va. Cav.

Brooke, F. T., Staunton, Va., Pvt., McClanahan's Battery

Brooks, John F., Staunton, Va., Pvt., Co. L, 5th Va. Inf.

Brown, John M., Valley Mills, Va., Co. F, 5th Va. Inf.

Brown, Marshall H., Bridgeport, W.Va., Pvt., Co. D, 10th Va. Inf.

Brown, S. Allen, Staunton, Va., Co. C, 14th Va. Cav.

Brownlee, E. G., Philadelphia, Pa., Pvt., McClanahan's Battery

Brownlee, J. A., Waynesboro, Va., Pvt., Co. H, 4th Va. Inf.

Brubeck, A. S., Staunton, Va., Pvt., Co. D, 25th Va. Inf.

Bryan, James W., AACS Charter member

Bucher, C. D., Augusta Co., Va.; Pvt., Co. A, 1st Va. Cav.

Bucher, Milton William, Augusta Co., Va., Pvt., Co. L, 5th Va. Inf.

Bumgardner, James Alexander, Greenville, Va., Ord. Sgt., Marquis' Battery

Bumgardner, James, Jr., Staunton, Va., Captain & Adj., Co. F, 5th Va. Inf., AACS Charter Pres

Bumgardner, W. L., Pvt., Co. E, 1st Va. Cav., AACS Charter member

Burke, Thomas, Staunton, Va., Pvt., Quartermaster's Dept.

Burruss, Wilson M., Staunton, Va., Pvt., Caroline Artillery

Byers, Samuel, Burketown, Va., Pvt., Opie's Co., Davis Bttn. Cav./courier for Gen. Jones

Byrd, John T., Williamsville, Va., Capt., Co. E, 18th Va. Cav.

Cale, Jacob B., Middlebrook, Va., Pvt., Co. H, 5th Va. Inf.

Cameron, John Hyde, Goshen, Va., Adj., 18th Va. Cav.

Campbell, Mathew J., Rockbridge Co., Va., Pvt., Co. E, 5th Va. Inf.

Carrier, M. E., Staunton, Va., Pvt., Co. H, 10th Va. Inf.

Carroll, George Franklin, Staunton, Va., Pvt., Co. D, 5th Va. Inf.

Carroll, John M., Staunton, Va., Pvt., Co. L, 5th Va. Inf.

Catlett, R. H., Staunton, Va., Major & A.A. Gen., Gen. John Echols' Brigade

Cease, John Worthington, Staunton, Va., Pvt., Co. L, 5th Va. Inf.

Chrisman, Levi, Augusta Co., Va., Pvt., Co. A, 52nd Va. Inf.

Chrisman, T. F., Augusta Co., Va., Pvt., Co. A, 52nd Va. Inf.

Clemner, George Lewis, Jr., Swoope, Va., Pvt, 2nd Co. I, 62nd Va. Inf.

Cline, John W., Staunton, Va., Pvt., Co. L, 5th Va. Inf.

Coalter, Mathew R., Deerfield, Va., Pvt., Co. E, 27th Va. Inf.

Cochran, George M., Jr., Staunton, Va., QM, 52nd Va. Inf., AACS Charter member

Coffelt, John B., Staunton, Va., Pvt., Co. B, 7th Va. Cav.

Coiner, C. J., Swoope, Va., Pvt., Co. C, 43rd Bttn. Va. Cav.

Coleman, Samuel H., Roanoke, Va., 1st Lt., Garber's Staunton Artillery, AACS Charter member

Collins, William B., Staunton, Va., Courier, Quartermaster's Dept.

Cook, J. W., Augusta Co., Pvt., Co. D, 52nd Va. Inf.

Coiner, Cyrus B., Fishersville, Va., Capt., Co. G, 52nd Va. Inf.

Coiner, C. J., Swoope, Va., Pvt., Co. C, 43rd Bttn. Va. Cav.

Crawford, Charles Edward, Ft. Defiance, Va., Pvt., Co. E, 1st Va. Cav.

Crawford, John D., New Hope, Va., Lt., Co. I, 7th Va. Cav.

Crawford, William Bell, Mt. Meridian, Va., 1st Cpl., Co. E, 1st Va. Cav.

Creigh, Cyrus, Staunton, Va., Pvt., Co. B, 60th Va. Inf.

Crogan, R. R., Staunton, Va., Color bearer, 1st Md. Cav.

Cunningham, Solomon, Staunton, Va., Pvt., Co. K, 62nd Va. Inf.

Cushing, E. M., Staunton, Va., Pvt., Quartermaster's Dept.

Daingerfield, L. P., Staunton, Va., Pvt., Bath Cav., 11th Bttn. Va. Cav.

Doyle, T. S., Pvt., Co. C, 5th Va. Inf., AACS Charter member

Drake, David William, Staunton, Va., Sgt. Major, Co. L, 5th Va. Inf & Co. E, 1st Va. Cav.

Drumheller, William P., Staunton, Va., Pvt., Co. H, 27th Va. Inf.

Dunlap, James Logan, West View, Sgt., Co. F, 5th Va. Inf.

Dunlap, Samuel A., Augusta Co., Va., Pvt., Co. B, 14th Va. Cav.

Echols, John, Staunton, Va., Brig. Gen., Dept. of SW Va.

Elder, Thomas C., Staunton, Va., Major & Commissary, Perry's Florida Brigade

Engleman, W. Dan, Greenville, Va., Pvt., 36th Bttn. Va. Cav.

Ervine, John V., Staunton, Va., 1st Sgt., Co. E, 31st Va. Inf.

Evans, George R., Staunton, Va., Pvt., Co. E, 28th Va. Inf.

Fauber, John H., Waynesboro, Va., Drummer, Co. H, 5th Va. Inf.

Fauver, J. A., Staunton, Va., Lt., Co. F, 52nd Va. Inf., AACS Charter member

Fauver, James Henry, Augusta Co., Va., Pvt., Co. I, 5th Va. Inf.

Finley, George W., Tinkling Spring, Va., Capt., Co. K, 56th Va. Inf.

Fishburne, E. G., Waynesboro, Va., Sgt., Co. E, 1st Va. Cav.

Fishburne, George W., Staunton, Va., Pvt., Co. C, 14th Va. Cav.

Fitch, George Washington, Greenville, Va., Pvt., Co. E, 5th Va. Inf.

Fonerdan, Clarence, Maryland, Pvt., Co. A, 27th Va. Cav. & Carpenter's Battery

Foster, James, Valley Mills, Va., Pvt., Co. H, 5th Va. Inf.

Freed, William A., Waynesboro, Va., Pvt., Co. E, 1st Va. Cav.

Fretwell, William West, Staunton, Va., Pvt., Co. L, 5th Va. Inf.

Fulcher, E. A., Staunton, Va., Capt., Co. A, 10th Va. Cav./AACS Charter Board of Mgrs.

Fuller, J. M., Staunton, Va., Sgt., Co. D, 4th Va. Inf.

Fultz, Alex. H., Staunton, Va., Capt., Staunton Artillery/AACS Charter member

Funsten, Oliver R., Jr., Staunton, Va., 1st Lt./Adj., 11th Va. Cav., AACS Charter member

Furr, James H., Staunton, Va., Pvt., Co. D, 5th Va. Inf.

Garrett, J. A., Staunton, Va., Pvt., Co. I, 2nd Kentucky Cav.

Gay, Henry Erskine, Staunton, Va., Pvt., Charlottesville & Rockbridge Battery

Gibson, Dr. J. St. P., Staunton, Va., Surgeon, 52nd Va. Inf.

Gibson, J. W., Staunton, Va., Pvt., Co. C, 52nd Va. Inf.

Gibson, W. W., Staunton, Va., Pvt., Staunton Artillery

Giles, S. N., Raphine, Va., Pvt., Co. G, 7th Va. Cav.

Gilkeson, John W., Mint Spring, Va., Lt., Co. D, 25th Va. Inf.

Gilkeson, William Grattan, Mint Spring, Va., Pvt., Co. F, 5th Va. Inf.

Gooch, G. G., Staunton, Va., Pvt., Co. A, 13th Va. Inf., AACS Charter member

Gorman, William H., Staunton, Va., Pvt., 1st Maryland Artillery

Granger, Jacob F., Staunton, Va., Pvt., Co. D, 2nd Va. Inf.

Grattan, Charles, Staunton, Va., Capt., Ordinance Dept., 2nd Corps

Gregory, Charles E., Staunton, Va., Pvt., Co. L, 5th Va. Inf.

Greiner, David M., Folly Mills, Va., Pvt., Co. C, 5th Va. Inf.

Greiner, E. G. M., Staunton, Va., Pvt., Co. H, 14th Va. Cav.

Guy, R.M., Staunton, Va., Pvt., Quartermaster's Dept.

Haldeman, Martin Asher, Rolla, Va., Pvt., Co. C, 5th Va. Inf.

Hamilton, Augustus Houston, Steele's Tavern, Pvt., Chapman's Battery & Rockbridge Art.

Hamilton, Robert Allen, Staunton, Va., Pvt., Co. A, 5th Va. Inf./ AACS Charter Board

Hamilton, W. W., Middlebrook, Va., Pvt., Co. E, 1st Va. Cav.

Hanger, Jacob A., Staunton, Va., Pvt., Co. I, 14th Va. Cav.

Hanger, J. Marshall, Augusta Co., Va., Major/AQM, Gen. J. E. B. Stuart's Staff, AACS VP & Charter member

Harman, Lewis, Staunton, Va., Adj. & Capt., Co. I, 12th Va. Cav./ AACS Charter member

Harnesberger, George W., Sewell, W.Va., Pvt., Co. I, 5th Va. Inf.

Harris, C. T., Annex, Va., Pvt., 12th Va. Cav.

Harris, James W., Fishersville, Va., Pvt., Co. H, 5th Va. Inf.

Harris, John R., Staunton, Va., Pvt., Co. B, 23rd Va. Cav.

Hart, Alex, Norfolk, Va., Major, Co. D, 5th Louisiana Inf., AACS Charter member

Harvey, James Alexander, Greenville, Va., Pvt., Co. E, 5th Va. Inf.

Hays, John W., Greenville, Va., Pvt., Co. E, 5th Va. Inf.

Henkel, M. J., Mt. Sidney, Va., Pvt., McClanahan's Battery

Henkel, S. H., Staunton, Va., Pvt., Co. H, 12th Bttn. Va. Cav.

Henry, Hugh W., Staunton, Va., Capt., Co. K, 22nd Alabama Inf.

Hensell, Edward L., Mint Spring, Va., Pvt., Co. B, 2nd Va. Inf.

Henton, D. B., Fort Defiance, Va., Pvt., Co. I, 14th Va. Cav.

Hicks, J. D., Stuarts Draft, Va., Pvt., Co. H, 2nd Va. Inf.

Hite, Henry C., Staunton, Va., Pvt., 39th Bttn. Va. Cav.

Hoover, J. M., Adlai, Va., Pvt., Marquis Battery

Holt, Charles Asbury, Staunton, Va., Capt., Co. K, 62nd Va. Inf., AACS Charter member

Hopewell, John William, Mt. Solon, Va., Pvt., Co. I, 5th Va. Inf.

Hosey, R. F., Staunton, Va., Pvt., Grove's Battery

Hotchkiss, Jedediah, Staunton, Va., Major & Topographical Engineer, Stonewall Jackson's Staff, AACS Charter Board

Houseman, Joseph, Staunton, Va., Pvt., Latham's Battery

Houser, William Steele, Greenville, Va., Pvt., Co. E, 5th Va. Inf.

Huffer, William, Mt. Solon, Co. C, 18th Va. Cav.

Hughart, James P., Sewell, W.Va., Capt., Co. D, 62nd Va. Inf.

Hullihen, Walter Q. (Rev.), Staunton, Va., aide de camp for Gen. J. E. B. Stuart & Capt. /AACS Charter member and A.A. Genl. For Gen. L. Lomax's Brigade

Hupman, David A., Augusta Co., Va., Co. I, 5th Va. Inf.

Hupman, John A., Staunton, Va., Pvt., Co. A, 52nd Va. Inf.

Hupman, G. T., Kansas City, Mo., Pvt., Co. A, 52nd Va. Inf.

Hutcheson, George Anderson, Staunton, Va., Pvt., Co. E, 5th Va. Inf., AACS Charter Board

Hutcheson, James Alexander, Staunton, Va., Pvt., Co. E, 5th Va. Inf.

Hyer, Henry H., Staunton, Va., Pvt., Co. L, 5th Va. Inf., AACS Charter member

Johnston, Jerry, Staunton, Va., Pvt., Co. H, 25th Va. Inf.

Kable, William Hartman, Staunton, Va., Capt., Co. F, 10th Va. Cav.

Keiser, George Franklin, Greenville, Va., Lt., Co. H, 5th Va. Inf.

Keller, Henry Swoope, Augusta Co., Va., Pvt., Co. F, 5th Va. Inf.

Kennedy, James Samuel, Waynesboro, Va., Pvt., Co. H, 5th Va. Inf.

Ker, James, Sr., Staunton, Va., Capt., Gen. R. S. Ewell's Staff

Kerr, D. M., New Hope, Va., Pvt., Co. E, 1st Va. Cav.

Kerr, Gerard B., Cadiz, Ohio, Pvt., Co. L, 5th Va. Inf.

Kerr, James T., New Hope, Va., Pvt., Co. E, 1st Va. Cav.

Kerr, John S., Laurel Hill, Va., Pvt., Co. E, 1st Va. Cav.

Kerr, Samuel H., Waynesboro, Va., Pvt., Co. E, 1st Va. Cav.

Kerr, Wesley S., Staunton, Va., Pvt., McClanahan's Battery

Kidd, John W., Staunton, Va., Pvt., Co. K, 11th Va. Inf.

Kinney, E. C., Staunton, Va., Pvt., McClanahan's Battery

Kinney, John Marshall, Staunton, Va., Pvt., Ordinance Dept.

Kirby, J. L. S., Staunton, Va., Capt., Co. H, 4th Regt. Engineer Trans-Missisippi

Koiner, Kasper Benton, Koiner's Store, Va., Pvt., Co. H, 5th Va. Inf.

Lawrence, James Welsey, Staunton, Va., Pvt., Staunton Artillery

Leftwich, R. T., Staunton, Va., Pvt., Co. H, 9th Va. Cav.

Leonard, John F., Waynesboro, Va., Pvt., Co. E, 1st Va. Cav.

Leonard, M. L., Waynesboro, Va., Pvt., Co. E, 1st Va. Cav.

Lessley, James A. H., Buffalo Gap, Va., Pvt., Co. D, 5th Va. Inf.

Lewis, James A., Staunton, Va., Pvt., Co. B, 10th Va. Inf.

Lightner, John Samuel, Lofton, Va., Pvt., Co. E, 5th Va. Inf.

Lightner, W., Swoope, Va., Enrolling agent, Capt. Avis' Co.

Lilley, John D., Greenville, Va., Lt. Col., 52nd Va. Inf./AACS Charter Board

Lohr, James Madison, Staunton, Va., Pvt., Co. L, 5th Va. Inf.

Long, George W., Staunton, Va., Pvt., Staunton Artillery

Long, John T., Staunton, Va., Pvt., Staunton Artillery/AACS Charter member

Long, W. J., Staunton, Va., Pvt., Staunton Artillery

Loyd, Patrick, Augusta Co., Pvt., Co. F, 52nd Va. Inf.

MacFarland, James Nathaniel, Sgt., Co. E, 5th Va. Inf.

McCorkle, John S., Staunton, Va., Pvt. Kilpatrick's Battery

McAllister, Richard, Augusta Co., Pvt., Southall's Battery

McAllister, William M., Warm Springs, Va., Sgt., Carpenter's Battery

McCane, James N., Bridgeport, W.Va., Pvt., Harrison Guard

McCullough, S. T., Staunton, Va., Lt., Co. D, 2nd Md. Inf.

McCune, R. H., Kansas City, Mo., Pvt., Co. D, 18th Va. Inf.

McCutchan, James Yates, Pvt., Co. D, 5th Va. Inf.

McCutchan, James Robert, Staunton, Va., Pvt., Co. D, 5th Va. Inf.

McFarland, James Nathaniel, Staunton, Va., Lt., Co. E, 5th Va. inf., AACS Board of Managers Charter

McIlhaney, Hugh Milton, Staunton, Va., 1st Sgt., Co. F, 43rd Bttn. Va. Cav. /AACS Charter member

McManaway, James, Middlebrook, Va., Co. D, 5th Va. Inf.

McNair, James N., Chruchville, Va., Pvt., Co. F, 5th Va. Inf.

McPheeters, R. P., Mint Springs, Va., Pvt., Co. C, 39th Bttn. Va. Cav.

Manley, Berry, Middlebrook, Va., Pvt., Co. D, 5th Va. Inf.

Marr, William T., Staunton, Va., Pvt., Moorman's Battery Stuart Horse Artillery

Marquis, J. C., Staunton, Va., Captain Marquis Battery, Reserve Artillery, AACS Charter member

Mason, Bingley Jackson, Staunton, Va., Pvt., Co. B, 33rd Va. Inf.

Matthews, J. M., Staunton, Va., Pvt., O. D, 19th Va. Inf.

May, George W., Staunton, Va., Pvt., Co. A, 12th Va. Inf.

Miller, David F., Moffat's Creek, Va., Pvt., Co. D, 5th Va. Inf.

Miller, G. Crawford, Ft. Defiance, Va., Pvt., Co. E, 1st Va. Cav.

Miller, J. Mason, Jr., Staunton, Va., Pvt., Co. K, 33rd Texas Cav.

Miller, M. Erskine, Staunton, Va., Pvt., Co. D, 44th Texas Inf.

Minor, Berkeley, Staunton, Va., Pvt., Rockbridge Artillery

Mitchell, T. J., Staunton, Va., Pvt., Co. G, 7th Va. Inf.

Mohler, J. L., Shendun, Va., Pvt., Co. B, 10th Va. Inf.

Mohler, H. W., Shendun, Va., Pvt., Hospital Steward 2nd Corps

Moon, E. R., Fisherville, Va., Pvt., 2nd Co. B, 25th Va. Inf., AACS Charter member

Moorman, William H., Ft. Defiance, Va., Pvt., Opie's Co., Davis Bttn. Cav.

Moran, T. K., Crozet, Va., Pvt., Co. D, 14th Va. Inf.

Morton, Thomas C., Staunton, Va., Capt., Co. F, Edgar's Battalion, 1st Va. Brigade, Breckinridge's Division

Murray, J. Ogden, Goshen, Va., Major, Wise's Battalion

Neal, Cyrus S., Staunton, Va., Pvt., Co. I, 27th Va. Inf.

Newman, Joseph A., Staunton, Va., Pvt., Staunton Artillery/AACS Charter member

Newman, W. R., Staunton, Va., Pvt., Staunton Artillery

Newton, James W., Staunton, Va., Major, 5th Va. Inf.

O'Brien, Maurice, Augusta Co., Va., Pvt., Co. F, 5th Va. Inf.

Olimans, C. W., Staunton, Va., Pvt., Co. D, 5th La. Inf.

Olivier, Warner L., Staunton, Va., Sgt., Pegram's Battery/AACS Charter Sec. & Treas.

Opie, John Newton, Staunton, Va., Co. L, 5th Va. Inf. & AACS Charter member

Pace, T. A., Staunton, Va., Pvt., Co. F, 21st Va. Inf.

Palmer, Henry Clay, Greenville, Va., Pvt., Co. B, 10th Va. Inf.

Pancake, John Silas, Staunton, Va., Pvt., Co. D, 11th Va. Cav. & 13th Cav.

Parker, John W. B., Pvt., Co. C, 17th Va. Inf.

Patterson, Alex Lee, Augusta Co., Va., Pvt., Co. C, 43rd Bttn. Va. Cav.

Patterson, J. A., Waynesboro, Va., Capt., Co. A, 52nd Va. Inf./AACS Charter VP

Patterson, S. N., Harriston, Va., Cpl., Co. A, 52nd Va. Inf.

Patterson, William C., Sherando, Va., Pvt., Co. B, 23rd Va. Cav.

Patterson, W. W., Augusta Co., Va., Pvt., Co. C, 43rd Bttn. Va. Cav.

Peaco, George W., Staunton, Va., Pvt., Co. D, 20th Va. Inf.

Pearson, John T., Augusta Co., Va., Pvt., Co. B, 19th Va. Inf.

Peer, John, Staunton, Va., Pvt., McClanahan's Battery

Pilson, Samuel F., Staunton, Va., Orderly Sgt., Co. B, 23rd Va. Cav.

Piper, George A., Staunton, Va., Pvt., Co. A, 39th Bttn. Va. Cav.

Plunkett, Lysander H., Staunton, Va., Color Cpl., Co. E, 5th Va. Inf.

Porterfield, John F., Staunton, Va., Co. H, 5th Va. Inf.

Powers, George W., Augusta Co., Va., Pvt., Co. G, 5th Va. Inf.

Powers, Henry Mitchell, Staunton, Va., Co. G, 5th Va. Inf.

Pratt, G. Julian, Capt., Co. H, 18th Va. Cav., AACS Charter Board

Proctor, N. R., Staunton, Va., Pvt., Co. B, 12th Va. Cav.

Quarles, M. W., Basic City, Va., Pvt., Co. F, 4th Va. Cav.

Rader, W. H., Durango, Colo., Pvt. Co. E, 1st Va. Cav.

Ransom, Thomas D., Staunton, Va., Capt. of scouts secret service dept, cav. corps/AACS Charter VP

Rawlings, B. C., Raphine, Va., Pvt., Co. D, 30th Va. Inf.

Riddleberger, Elias, Ft. Defiance, Va., Pvt., Co. L, 5th Va. Inf. & 5th Cavalry

Robertson, J. S., Spottswood, Va., Pvt., Staunton, Artillery

Roden, James Benedict, Waynesboro, Va., Pvt., Co. C/E, 7th Louisiana Infantry

Roller, C. A., Staunton, Va., Pvt., Co. E, 1st Va. Cav.

Roller, Charles Summerville, Ft. Defiance, Va., Pvt., Co. E, 1st Va. Cav.

Ruebush, John S., Mt. Sidney, Va., Pvt., Co. D, 37th Va. Inf.

Ruff, Joseph S., Staunton, Va., Pvt., Co. H, 16th Va. Cav.

Rusmisell, W. H. H., Staunton, Va., Pvt., Co. C, 52nd Va. Inf.

Schmucker, George E., Staunton, Va., Pvt., Co. B, 33rd Va. Inf.

Schoppert, G. A., Augusta Co., Va., Pvt., Ordinance Dept.

Scott, John C., New Hope, Va., Courier, Cav. Corps, ANVa

Scott, W. N. (Rev.), Staunton, Va., Pvt., Co. D, 1st Va. Cav.

Shields, J. C., AACS Charter member

Shields, W. H., Greenville, Va., Pvt., Co. B, 23rd Va. Cav.

Silling, John Hendrew, Staunton, Va., Pvt., Co. I, 5th Va. Inf.

Silling, R. M., Staunton, Va., Pvt., Co. C, 14th Va. Cav.

Simpson, William Morton, Staunton, Va., 2nd Lt., Co. E, 17th Va. Inf./AACS Charter member

Skinner, James H., Staunton, Va., Col., 52nd Va. Inf. /AACS Charter member

Smiley, John Price, Middlebrook, Va., Pvt., Co. D, 5th Va. Inf.

Smiley, Thomas Martin, Moffat's Creek, Va., Captain, Co. D, 5th Va. Inf.

Smith, Joel N., Staunton, Va., Pvt., Co. E, 51st Va. Inf. & Co. B, 8th Va. Cav.

Smith, John B., Greenville, Va., Pvt., Co. E, 1st Va. Cav.

Smith, M. B., West Augusta, Va., McCausland's

Snyder, James A., Staunton, Va., Co. D, 5th Va. Inf.

Southards, James W., Staunton, Va., Pvt., Staunton Artillery

Spitler, Henry, Swoope, Va., Pvt., Co. F, 5th Va. Inf.

Spitler, Jared Wellington, Pvt, Co. C, 5th Va. Inf. & Co. I, 14th Va. Cav.

Sprinkle, John W., Staunton, Va., Pvt., Co. L, 5th Va. Inf.

Stitser, Jonas J., West Augusta, Va., Pvt., Co. I, 5th Va. Inf.

Stover, George H., Staunton, Va., Pvt., Co. E, 5th Va. Inf.

Stribling, F. T., Jr., Staunton, Va., Pvt., Chew's Battery Stuart Horse Artillery

Stump, Job H., Fishersville, Va., Pvt., Co. B, 1st Va. Cav.

Summerson, William Frazier, Staunton, Va., VMI Corps of Cadets

Swink, Calvin L., Waynesboro, Va., Pvt., Co. E, 1st Va. Cav.

Taliaferro, William B., Jennings Gap, Va., Pvt., Co. H, 5th Va. Inf.

Tankesley, William M., Augusta Co., Va., Pvt., Co. G, 5th Va. Inf.

Templeton, James A., Staunton, Va., Co. H, 52nd Va. Inf.

Terrill, John W., Basic City, Va., pvt., Co. B, 52nd Va. Inf.

Thacker, Green M., Staunton, Va., Pvt., Co. E, 1st Va. Cav.

Timberlake, Stephen D., Staunton, Va., Pvt., Co. B, 12th Va. Cav.

Timberlake, Seth M., Fishersville, Va., Co. G, 2nd Va. Inf.; 1st Sgt./Ord. Sgt., Co. B, 12th Va. Cav.

Tribbett, A. D., Valley Mills, Va., Pvt., Co. H, 27th Va. Inf.

Trotter, James H., Staunton, Va., Pvt., Signal Corps and Va. Cav.

Walker, James A., Wytheville, Va., Brig. Gen., Stonewall Brigade

Walker, S. H., Ft. Defiance, Va., 1st Lt., Co. E, 1st Va. Cav.

Waller, William Dabney, Staunton, Va., Capt. & Adj., 36th Bttn. Va. Cav.

Walter, Frederick W., Staunton, Va., Pvt., Co. A, Cobb's Georgia Legion Cav.

Waters, James Hurley, Staunton, Va., Capt., Co. L, 5th Va. Inf., AACS Charter member

Wayman, E. F., Staunton, Va., Pvt., Co. C, 43rd Bttn. Va. Cav.

Wayte, J. Newton, Staunton, Va., Asst. Surgeon, 62nd Virginia Infantry

Weir, Alexander H., Augusta Co., Va., Pvt., Co. H, 14th Va. Cav., AACS Charter member

Weller, Charles L., Staunton, Va., Capt., Co. C, 52nd Va. Inf., AACS Charter member

Weller, W. Frank, Staunton, Va., Pvt., Co. E, 1st Va. Cav.

Weller, William H., Staunton, Va., Pvt., Co. B, 39th Bttn. Va. Cav.

Whitesell, James P., Rockville, Ind., Pvt., McClanahan's Battery

Whitesell, John W., Staunton, Va., Pvt., Co. B, Albemarle Rifles, 19th Va. Inf.

Wholey, William S., Staunton, Va., Ordnance Sgt., Co. L, 5th Va. Inf./AACS Charter member

Wilkerson, Anthony P., Verona, Va., Pvt., Co. I, 5th Va. Inf.

Williams, Hazael Johnston, Greenville, Va., Col., 5th Va. Inf.

Williams, L. E., Staunton, Va., Pvt., Co. D, 6th Va. Cav.

Wilson, D. N., Churchville, Va., Pvt., Co. I, 14th Va. Cav.

Wilson, Peter Eidson, Staunton, Va., Capt., Co. F, 5th Va. Inf., AACS Charter member

Wingfield, W. H., Basic City, Va., Pvt., Co. A, 7th Va. Cav.

Woodward, P. H., Staunton, Va., Co. H, 10th Va. Inf.

Woodward, Thomas Doak, Staunton, Va., Pvt., Co. L, 5th Va. Inf.

Wright, John Alexander, Arbor Hill, Va., Pvt., Co. E, 5th Va. Inf.

Young, Charles E., Staunton, Va., Lt., Engineer Corps

Zirkle, Casper K., Staunton, Va., Sgt., W. H. Rice's Co. Arty.; Pvt., Ordinance Dept.

Honorary Members:

Daniel, Hon. John Warwick, Lynchburg, Va., Major on Gen. Early's Staff

Hunton, Eppa, Warrenton, Va., Brig. Gen. Hunton's Brigade

Lee, Fitzhugh, Richmond, Va., Maj. Gen. Lee's Div. Cav.

Lacy, Rev. Beverly Tucker, Alexandria, Va., Stonewall Jackson's Staff

Lanham, Gov. Samuel W., Austin, Texas, Sgt., S.C. Troops

McGuire, Hunter, Richmond, Va., Surgeon Medical Director, 2nd Corps, ANVa.

Smith, Rev. J. P., Richmond, Va., Aide, Stonewall Jackson's Staff

White, Rev. Henry M., Winchester, Va., Chaplain, ANVa.

** Note that "AACS" indicates previous membership with the Augusta Association of Confederate Survivors.*

Appendix B

Augusta County Confederate Disability or Artificial Limb Applicants (1882–1886)

The Virginia General Assembly enacted legislation, effective in 1867 and ending in 1894, to provide artificial limbs and other disability benefits to Virginia veterans of the Civil War.

To coordinate the program, and oversee the distribution of aid, the Assembly established the Board of Commissioners on Artificial Limbs. Injured soldiers submitted certificates from their county court stating that they were Virginia citizens, that they had lost a limb or had been otherwise disabled in the war, and what assistance they required. The veterans listed the command in which they served; included information on when, where, and how they were wounded; and provided details about their medical history.

These disability applications provide a strong sense of the Civil War's impact on individuals, families, and communities. In truth, many veterans found the postwar battle for economic survival and physical mobility nearly as difficult as the war itself.

1882

Baylor, John M.
Cook, James F.
Dangerfield, Leroy
Ross, William H.
Thornton, Jacob P.
VanLear, James P.
Wilkerson, Anthony P.
Zimmerman, Jacob

1883

Alexander, George
Bailey, William D.
Becks, George H.
Gamble, William H.
Keiser, Jeremiah
Kennedy, James S.
Kirby, Obediah
McGrath, Patrick
Patterson, John

1884

Ashley, J. A.
Bateman, Elijah
Bell, W. J.
Brown, Elisha B.
Carrel, Samuel.
Cease, John W.
Coffelt, John B.
Cook, John W.
Cosby, H. P.
Depriest, R. H.
Dickerson, Henry P.
Fauber, John H.
Fisher, Henry
Fry, Newton A.
Furr, George H.
Gorman, William H.
Granger, Jacob F.
Grooms, Arthur T.
Hanger, W. A.
Harris, James A.
Harris, John W.
Humphreys, James
Humphreys, Nathaniel
Lightner, John S.
Mayfield, Andrew J.
McGrath, Patrick
Painter, John F.
Patterson, Samuel N.
Rhoades, J. M.
Robson, John S.

Schindel, John H.
Sheets, Jacob
Shumaker, Joseph P.
Sidus, William A.
Snead, Parkes E.
Spiers, George
Taliaferro, John M.
Terrell, John W.
Tolley, William H.
Trout, James R.
Tutwiler, Joseph L.
VanFossin, W. H.
Whitesell, John W.
Wilkinson, A. P.
Wise, John H.
Wiseman, Elijah M.
Womeldorf, James A.
Womeldorf, John A.
Wormeldorf, John A.

1886

Almarode, George H.
Amis, James B.
Andrew, James M.
Argenbright, James S.
Baylor, John M.
Bear, Henry C.
Breeden, J. C.
Brown, James M.
Byers, R. G.
Mathews, Abraham
Moore, George
Vanfossen, William E.
VanLear, Ausbert G. L.
Way, James S.
Whitesell, William S.
Whitesell, John W.
Wilson, Samuel

Appendix C

Augusta County Confederate Veteran and Widow Pensioners 1888–1902

1888

Aldhiger, Nancy C.
Almarode, George H.
Alvis, Elizabeth
Anderson, Margaret E.
Apple, William H.
Argonbright, James S.
Armentrout, Charles E.
Bartley, V. C.
Bateman, Elijah
Bear, Fannie J.
Beard, Sarah J.
Blakemore, John F.
Blizzard, M. V.
Breeden, J. C.
Bright, Eueline
Brown, Elisha B.
Brown, James E.
Brown, Rebecca A.
Bryan, James Berkeley
Buchanan, John W.
Byers, Robert G.
Campbell, Andrew B.
Carroll, Mary A.
Cash, James
Clark, Lucy H.
Clarke, Frances M.
Collins, Mary L.
Cook, John W.
Curry, Diana A.
Curry, Nancy Virginia
Daingerfield, Leroy P.
Denis, Margaret A.
Depriest, Robert H.
Dickerson, H. B.
Dinkle, Caroline
Dull, Jacob H.
Dull, Jane R.
Edwards, Judith
Fisher, John A.
Furr, George H.
Gabbert, J. J.
Glenn, Barbara Catharine
Good, Rosana R.
Greiner, Rebecca
Griener, Ann W.
Grogan, R. R.
Grooms, Arthur T.
Hahn, Elizabeth
Hall, Martin
Harman, Ithamer R.
Harris, Daniel W.
Harris, James A.
Harris, James F.
Hawkins, John
Hemp, Sarah C.
Henderson, Rebecca F.
Hight, Nancy Ellen
Holbert, William T.
Houser, David S.
Humphrey, Susan B.
Humphreys, James F.
Humphreys, Nathaniel
Humphreys, William P.
Jones, Frances S.
Kennedy, James S.
King, Mary Ann
Lilly, John D.
Loyd, Patrick
Lucas, Ann E.
Marion, Frances
Masincup, Susan C.
Mathews, Abram
Mayfield, Andrew J.
Mays, Isaiah M.
McCormick, Eliza V.
McCutchan, Susan C.
Meek, John M.
Miller, Susan A.
Monroe, William H.
Montgomery, James H.
Moore, George E.
Painter, J. F.
Patterson, Rebecca
Perry, Robert B.
Poague, Sarah A.
Pross, Martha Ann
Ramsey, Sarah Jane
Read, Richard W.
Rhodes, James M.
Rife, Archibald S.
Roberts, Albert
Robinson, William J.
Rosen, Minerva F.
Ruebush, Sarah H.
St. Myer, William
Schindel, John H.
Sheets, Mary C.
Sherman, Margaret H.
Siders, William A.
Small, Sarah Jane
Smallwood, Mary Ann
Smith, Sarah A.
Smith, William C.
Snead, Parkes E.
Snead, William Elisha
Spiers, George
Spotts, Mary J.
Stagdale, John H.
Stover, Elizabeth J.
Stover, Joshua H.
Taliaferro, J. M.
Talley, Catharine
Talley, Margaret A.
Tayler, Emily
Taylor, William C.
Terrell, James
Terrell, John W.
Thompson, Sarah J.
Thornton, Jacob P.
Tisdale, Ann
Trout, James R.
Vance, Sarah C.
Vanfossen, William
Walker, Barbara G.
Wameldorf, John A.
Way, James S.
Weaver, John
Weever, Michael
Whitesell, Benjamin H.
Whitesell, John W.
Whitlock, Sarah F.
Wichael, Daniel
Wilkinson, A. P.
Wilson, Margaret P.
Wiseman, Elijah M.
Wiseman, Nancy
Zimmerman, Jacob H.

1900

Alexander, Sarah A.
Alford, Lavina
Allison, William H.
Armentrout, Charles E.
Baker, Ann E.
Bare, Henry C.
Bear, Henry C.
Beard, James E.
Biby, Henry G.
Blakemore, William S.
Bridge, Alexander
Brooks, George W.
Brooks, Robert T.
Byram, John T.
Bryant, Chas. P.
Byers, J. B.
Childress, D. D.
Childress, P. H.
Childress, William M.
Childress, William
Coffey, Edmund F.
Craig, David T.
Crizer, J. Lewis
Croft, Elizabeth
Echard, John
Elliott, Caroline E.
Faber, John H.
Fishburn, George W.

Fitzgerald, Robert W.
Fix, Elizabeth
Fix, W. J.
Gabbert, Magaret M.
Garrison, Jacob S.
Gibson, John B.
Gibson, John W.
Harris, James W.
Harris, John
Hays, Nancy
Hight, Lucinda B.
Hoffman, Christian
Holbert, William T.
Hoover, C. C.
Huff, Daniel
Hughart, Charles H.
Humphries, John B.
Huntley, Robert J.
Hupman, Lewis J.
Kesterson, S. B.
Loving, John W.
Manley, Berry
Mason, B. J.
McClung, Thomas W.
McGuffin, John W.
McLain, A. S.
Mitchell, T. J.
Pannell, George W.
Patterson, William
Plunkett, Lysander H.
Ponton, Richard H.
Reed, Jane C.
Reese, John E.
Robertson, Stephen F.
Rosen, William H.
Rusmisell, Andrew S.
Rusmisell, William H. H.
Ryan, Oliver
Sheets, Sarah M.
Shover, Catherine
Shue, A. W.
Simbro, Robert
Smith, Margaret L.
Smith, William R.
Snead, J. William Elisha
Sprouse, Peter
Stickley, Mary A.
Swink, William S.
Swisher, William F.
Tankesley, William M.
Terrell, John W.
Thompson, A. W.
Tinsley, W. H.
Tucker, Samuel E.
Walton, Lucy A.
Weakley, Lydia C.
Weaver, John W.
Whitsell, Peter
Wilkerson, Anthony P.
Wiseman, Henry B.
Wiseman, Samuel

1902

Adkins, Andrew J.
Adkins, Elvira E.
Alexander, Franklin
Alexander, J. W.
Alexander, Samuel H.
Alford, James A.
Almarode, Simon H.
Almond, James W.
Altizer, Martisha
Anderson, Robert H.
Anderson, Robert J.
Andrew, John H.
Argenbright, George W.
Argenbright, James
Argenbright, Nancy A.
Armentrout, Frances A.
Armentrout, J. C.
Armstrong, Florence C.
Armstrong, H. C.
Arnold, A. V.
Atkins, Alexander B.
Bailey, D. M.
Bailey, Margaret C.
Bailey, Mary
Bailey, Rebecca B.
Bailey, Sarah A.
Baldwin, J. W.
Bare, Emma C.
Bare, John S.
Barker, J. G.
Baylor, J. Robert
Beach, Dabney
Beach, Sallie A.
Bear, Annie
Beard, Annie
Beard, Carrie F.
Beard, David East
Beard, Minnie B.
Beck, Andrew D. S.
Beck, Martha V.
Bell, F. M.
Bell, John V.
Benton, H. R.
Berry, Deniza A.
Biby, Rebecca J.
Bishop, Edward F.
Black, Calvin Luther
Black, Mary Margaret
Blackburn, Mary M.
Blizzard, Cynthia A.
Bosserman, George H.
Bosserman, James C.
Bowers, Hulda
Bradburn, Isabella F.
Bradburn, William A.
Brand, J. W.
Breeden, J. Susan
Brown, Elizabeth
Brown, Hiram
Brown, James P.
Brown, Martha E.
Brownlee, Bettie A.
Brownlee, John A.
Bryant, Amanda C.
Bryant, Savannah J.
Bucher, C. D.
Bucher, Clarissa E.
Bucher, Jane C.
Bucher, Milton W.
Buckner, Irene W.
Bumgardner, J. Alexander
Bunch, James
Burford, John W.
Burnett, W. W.
Byers, Elizabeth
Byers, James B.
Byers, Louisa J.
Campbell, A. W.
Campbell, Annie G.
Carichoff, L. A.
Carrico, Simeon
Carroll, Patrick
Carter, Margaret
Cash, D. S.
Cash, Elizabeth F.
Cason, Sarah A.
Cease, Elizabeth A.
Cease, J. W.
Cease, John W.
Chandler, Arelda.
Chandler, John D.
Chapman, George M.
Chrisman, Levi
Chrisman, Thomas F.
Christian, Rebecca G.
Clark, Lucy A.
Clatterbough, S. C.
Clements, Joseph H.
Clements, Lewis S.
Clements, Mary E.
Clements, W. J.
Coffee, Sarah M.
Coffman, Jefferson P.
Coffman, Maggie Walker
Cole, Harrison
Coleman, Dianna
Collins, Benjamin F.
Collins, Nancy E.
Comer, Sallie S. C. Haney
Conner, John
Conner, Maggie
Cook, Abraham
Cook, Mandy Jane
Cook, Margaret E.
Cook, Samuel
Cox, Alex H.
Cox, Mary E.
Cox, Mary F.
Craig, Annie
Craig, William
Creigh, Cyrus
Crickenberger, Jennie S.
Curd, Mary M.
Currier, Emaline
Currier, P. W. C.
Currier, Robert H.
Curry, Sarah A. M.
Davis, Fannie E.
Davis, Lucy A.
Dawson, Sallie M.
Dension, Margaret V.
Dension, W. H.
Dickenson, Robert
Dickerson, Mary E.
Dickson, Mary Ann
Dinkle, Caroline
Dodd, John J.
Dodd, Margaret A.
Doggy, Jonas F.
Doyle, John Merritt
Dunlop, J. Logan
Dunlop, Robert Bailey
Dunlop, Sue Ella
Durham, L. G.
Eavey, Daniel
Eavey, Mary J.
Eavey, Mollie J.
Effinger, John T.
Ellinger, W. H.
Emerson, S. H.
Emswiller, Louisa M.
Erskine, C. J.
Ervin, Lina G.
Estill, Robert K.
Fauver, Nannie C.
Ferguson, Annie A.
Fielding, James E.
Fishburne, Ella Van Lear
Fisher, W. T.
Fisher, Winnie E.
Fitch, Charles W.
Fitch, George W.
Fix, Susan Margaret
Foley, Samuel H.
Fortune, James A.
Fretwell, William A.
Frymer, Charlotte
Furr, James H.
Furr, Sarah Margaret
Gaddy, James C.
Garber, Elizbeth A.
Gardner, Darcus Jane
Gardner, R. W.
Garnett, Ann Elizabeth
Gay, Betty C.
Genivan, S. C.
Gentry, Mary L.
Gibson, Leveellen
Gibson, W. W.
Gilkeson, Mary J.
Gilkeson, S. J.
Gish, Florence Barclay

Glenn, E. M.
Good, John C.
Goodwin, Florence
Gordon, John
Greaver, Jacob R.
Greaver, James H.
Greaver, Margaret Eliza
Grove, S. F.
Gulley, G. A.
Gwin, J. C.
Haines, Sallie R.
Hall, Houston
Hall, T. H.
Hall, W. L.
Hamilton, Drusilla V.
Hamilton, Jacob P.
Hanger, A. Sanford
Hanger, B. Nettie
Hanger, Catherine J.
Hanger, Eliza C.
Hanger, James F.
Hanger, John A.
Hanger, William B.
Hanna, Mary H.
Harding, Martha A. E.
Harlow, Sallie Ellen
Harlow, T. W.
Harman, Delila J.
Harrell, William A.
Harris, Charles T.
Harris, Florence M.
Harris, J. Clifton
Harris, Martha J.
Harris, Ozillah F.
Harris, William H.
Heiser, Elizabeth R.
Heizer, John B.
Helmick, John E.
Helmick, William
Hewett, Mary E.
Hicks, Annie
Higgs, Nancy E.
Hildebrand, Mary E.
Hill, W. H.
Hinkel, Michael J.
Hise, Elizabeth M.
Hobson, William S.
Holbert, E. A.
Holder, James A.
Hoover, R. D.
Horn, F. E.
Horn, James P.
Horn, Mary M.
Howdyshell, Martha A.
Hudson, Joseph
Huff, J. C.
Huffer, William
Huffman, Ida
Hulvery, Elizabeth E.
Hulvey, Lewis L.
Humphreys, J. B.
Humphreys, Laura
Humphreys, Martha
Hunter, Robert H.
Huntley, Thomas W.
Hupman, Lewis V.
Hupman, Mary E.
Ingram, Catherine
Ingram, Hugh
Jennings, Susan G.
Johnson, Jacob
Jollette, Eliza J.
Jollette, James F.
Keller, Fannie J.
Kelley, H. J.
Kelley, M. A.
Kellison, C. W.
Kerr, David M.
Kerr, Grace P.
Kerr, John M.
Kesterson, Mary C.
Keyton, James W.
Keyton, James W.
Kidd, C. C.
Kidd, C. C.
Kidd, Laura L.
Kinney, William N.
Kiracofe, Ann E.
Kiser, Adam
Kline, John Samuel
Knopp, Mary
Knopp, Noah
Knott, C. S.
Knott, Lydia
Knott, Mary M.
Knott, W. M.
Komer, K. B.
Kunkle, W. S.
Lamb, John C.
Landes, Joseph D.
Lange, W. F.
Law, Stephen
Lawhorn, Willis
Lawrence, James W.
Lawrence, Mary E.
Leavell, Edmund G.
Leonard, Mary E.
Leonard, Sarah Jane
Lessley, Jack H.
Lightner, William T.
Long, Daniel W.
Long, Sarah A.
Lovegrove, Sarah A.
Lovegrove, William H.
Lovick, Alexander
Lowman, George J.
Lowman, J. A.
Loyd, Martha E.
Lynn, Frederick
Lytton, Albert W.
Manley, Sarah Ann
Marks, Robert S.
Marrs, Braxton D.
Massie, Z. T.
Maston, J. W.
Mawyer, Hardin Smith
Maybush, Augustus
Maybush, Margaret
McAllister, Martha J.
McClure, Susan R.
McClury, J. Frank
McCorkle, William A.
McCormick, William Henry
McCrary, William
McCutchan, J. Y.
McCutchen, James R.
McFall, H. B.
McFall, Magnolia
McGehee, Jacob Owen
McGhee, Mary
McKee, Mariam S.
McKee, Simon P.
McLain, Josephine
McLeer, Catharine
McManaway, Valary Ann
McMillen, S. H.
McNeal, Rebecca J.
Meek, Isabella Brown
Melton, John Wesley
Merritt, Margaret
Michael, Hudson S.
Miller, C. L.
Miller, Sarah C.
Mills, George H.
Mills, W. E.
Minnick, Lucinda
Mohler, J. R.
Mohler, John L.
Monroe, James B.
Moon, Edward R.
Moran, Margaret
Moran, William
Mountjoy, Bettie P.
Nettleton, Lula Hope
Newcomb, Henry A.
Newcomb, M. J.
Nichols, Josephine
Nimmo, Lourena
Ott, James S.
Owens, R. P.
Painter, Frances A.
Painter, James H.
Palmer, James
Palmer, Rebecca F.
Pannell, Adam
Pannell, Lucy Jane
Parsons, David M.
Patrum, Margaret J.
Patrum, R. N.
Patterson, William Marden
Paul, Martha I.
Paxton, James O.
Paxton, Mary E.
Payne, Henry H.
Pelter, Sampson
Pendleton, Annie M.
Pendleton, Charles M.
Perkins, James H.
Perry, Fannie H.
Perry, R. B.
Phillips, Lewis
Phillips, Sarah J.
Pifer, Margaret
Pleasants, Mary A.
Pleasants, P. B.
Porterfield, Jacob
Progs, Morgan
Propst, H. T.
Propst, Julia A.
Puffenbarger, Samuel
Quick, James R.
Ralston, Anna J.
Ralston, John H.
Ramsey, Jacob
Rankin, Maggie
Rankin, Thomas
Rawley, John H.
Rawley, Sarah E.
Reed, Tabitha Jane
Reeves, George W.
Rhodes, Bettie
Riddleberger, Elias
Rife, A. S.
Rimel, John P.
Risk, Mary D.
Ritchie, George Dallas
Ritchie, James K. P.
Roberts, John
Roberts, Sarah C.
Robertson, Frances A.
Robertson, J. S.
Robertson, J. W.
Robertson, Mariah J.
Rogers, Robert M.
Rohr, Jacob
Roller, Henrietta A.
Rosen, Minerva F.
Ross, Margaret A. E.
Ross, Pocahontas
Ross, William H.
Rossen, Malinda F.
Rowe, Amos
Rowe, Isabella
Rowe, James H.
Rowe, Susan S.
Runkle, C. R.
Runkle, Emma V.
Runnels, Virginia A.
Rusmiselle, George B.
Sandy, R. W.
Schindel, John H.
Seig, D. A.
Sellers, Mary E.
Sensabaugh, Mary J.

Shall, Henry
Sheets, Mary C.
Sheets, Mary D.
Sheets, Phoebe J.
Sheets, William W.
Sheets, William H.
Shomo, James C.
Shull, J. H.
Shull, Lucinda
Shull, Sarah J.
Shull, Sophronia F.
Shumate, Cornelia F.
Shumate, Thomas S.
Silling, Annie E.
Smith, Elizabeth F.
Smith, M. B.
Smith, Virginia
Snead, J. M.
Snead, Lucinda
Snead, Mary E.
Snead, Virginia F.
Snow, Thomas
Snyder, J. Robert
Snyder, James A.
Snyder, John R.
Snyder, Mary M.
Spitler, Eliza F.
Spitler, Henry
Spotts, Virginia P.
Spradlin, J. M.
Spradlin, Samuel S.
Sprouse, Ellen
Sprowl, Richard
Staten, Julia A.
Steele, A. H.
Stiegel, Sallie Jane
Stitzer, J. J.
Stitzer, Marshall
Stockdale, John H.
Stockdale, Lorena B.
Stomback, Sarah A.
Stoutamyer, G. W.
Stoutamyer, Mary E.
Strickler, John M.
Strickler, Rebecca Ann
Stridler, J. H.
Stuart, Jennie
Stump, John H.
Suddarth, Belle D.
Supple, Robert F.
Sutler, Joseph L.
Swartzel, Anna Steele
Swats, S. B.
Swats, Virginia C.
Sweet, Elizabeth
Swink, Calvin L.
Swink, M. J.
Taliaferro, W. B.
Talley, James A.
Talley, Martha Jane
Tanner, William.
Tanner, William
Taylor, Fannie Virginia
Taylor, G. W.
Taylor, Margaret Jane
Taylor, Robert
Taylor, Susan M.
Terrell, Mary
Terrell, R. H.
Tewalt, William
Thacker, Daniel
Thomas, Charles H.
Thomas, J. D.
Thomas, S. T.
Thompson, Catharine
Todd, Annie
Trainer, W. D.
Troxell, Mary J.
Van Lear, Madison P.
Van Pelt, Fannie
Van Tossen, Nannie J.
Varner, John P.
Vaughan, Madison P.
Via, William M.
Vigar, John E.
Vigar, M. J.
Vincent, Clara
Vincent, E. F.
Vines, James W.
Vint, Beniah
Waddelow, Rebecca M.
Wade, Martha E.
Wagner, Sarah E.
Wampler, B. F.
Wampler, Simon W.
Weaver, Catherine M.
Weaver, John
Weeks, Lucy F.
Welcher, Joseph
Weller, Nannie
Whitesell, Caroline J.
Whitesell, James W.
Whitesell, Mary M.
Whitmore, James B.
Whitmore, John S.
Whitmore, Susan.
Wieseman, Jerusha
Wilkerson, Mary C.
Willaims, Andrew
Williams, Bettie A.
Wilson, George W.
Wine, D. S.
Wiseman, Jacob F.
Wiseman, James F.
Wiseman, John B.
Wiseman, Mary E.
Wiseman, William E.
Witt, Sallie E.
Woodson, P. T.
Woodward, L. T.
Woodward, M. J.
Wright, Schuyler
Young, Lucy A.
Yount, J. W.
Yount, Virginia
Ziegler, A. E.
Zirkle, C. K.

Bibliography

Manuscripts

Library of Congress, Washington, D.C.
Jedediah Hotchkiss Papers.

Library of Virginia
Public Works Papers Pertaining to Turnpikes.

Roster of Confederate Pensioners of Virginia. Richmond, 1912, 1914, 1920, 1922, 1926.

National Archives, Washington, D.C.
Southern Claims Commission Records, Disallowed, Allowed, and Referred Claims for Augusta County, Virginia, 1871–1880.

Compiled Service Records for Union and Confederate Organizations.

Staunton Public Library
Genealogy and Local History Files

Work Projects Administration Historical Inventory of Augusta County, Virginia. n.p.

Virginia Military Institute Archives, Lexington, Va.
Alumni Records.

Waynesboro Public Library
"Waynesboro in Civil War Days"

Diary of DeWitt Clinton Gallaher, A Diary Depicting the Experiences of DeWitt Clinton Gallaher in the War Between the States While Serving in the Confederate Army

Newspapers

Staunton Spectator

Staunton News-Leader

Staunton Republican Vindicator

Rockingham Register

Published Resources

Allan, William. *History of the Campaigns of Gen. T .J. (Stonewall) Jackson in the Shenandoah Valley of Virginia.* Philadelphia, 1880.

Anderson, Paul Christopher. *Blood Image: Turner Ashby in the Civil War and the Southern Mind.* Baton Rouge, La., 2002.

Armstrong, Richard L. *7th Virginia Cavalry.* Lynchburg, Va., 1992.

———. *11th Virginia Cavalry.* Lynchburg, Va., 1989.

———. *The Battle of McDowell.* Lynchburg, Va., 1990.

———. *19th and 20th Virginia Cavalry.* Lynchburg, Va., 1994.

Augusta County, Virginia Heritage Book, Staunton, Va., 1998.

Augusta Historical Bulletin

Baylor, George. *Bull Run to Bull Run: Four Years in the Army of Northern Virginia Containing a Detailed Account of the Career and Adventures of the Baylor Light Horse, Company B, Twelfth Virginia Cavalry, C.S.A.,* Washington, D.C., 1983.

Beautiful Thornrose: Memorial Edition. Staunton, Va., 1921.

Beautiful Thornrose, Staunton, Va., 1907.

Bonnell, John C., Jr. *Sabres in the Shenandoah: The 21st New York Cavalry, 1863–1866.* Shippensburg, Pa., 1996.

Bowman, Curtis L., Sr. *Waynesboro Days of Yore,* Vol. 1. Waynesboro, Va., 1990.

———. *Waynesboro Days of Yore,* Vol. 2. Waynesboro, Va., 1992.

Brice, Marshall Moore. *Conquest of a Valley.* Charlottesville, Va., 1965.

———. *The Stonewall Brigade Band.* Verona, Va., 1967.

Brown, David J., ed. *Staunton Virginia: A Pictorial History.* Staunton, Va., 1985.

Bureau of the Census. 1860. Census records for Augusta County, Virginia.

Casler, John O. *Four Years in the Stonewall Brigade.* Guthrie, Okla., 1895.

Cavada, F. F. *Libby Life: Experiences as a Prisoner of War in Richmond, Va., 1863–64.* Philadelphia, 1864.

Chapla, John D. *50th Virginia Infantry.* Lynchburg, Va., 1997.

Civil War Times Illustrated

Clark, Champ. *Decoying the Yanks: Jackson's Valley Campaign.* Alexandria, Va.: Time-Life Books, 1984.

Collins, Darrell L. *The Battles of Cross Keys and Port Republic.* Lynchburg, Va., 1993.

Confederate Veteran. 40 vols. Nashville, Tenn.: Confederate Veteran, 1893–1932.

Cumulative Index to the Confederate Veteran Magazine, 1893–1932. 3 vols. Wilmington, N.C., 1986.

Dabney, Robert L. *Life and Campaigns of Lieut, Gen. Thomas J. Jackson.* New York, 1866.

———. *Discussions,* Vol. IV. Mexico, Mo., 1897.

Davis, William C. *The Battle of New Market.* Garden City, N.Y., 1975.

Delaughter, Roger U., Jr. *18th Virginia Cavalry.* Lynchburg, Va. 1985.

———. *McNeill's Rangers.* Lynchburg, Va., 1986.

Denison, Frederic. *Sabres and Spurs: The First Rhode Island Cavalry in the Civil War, 1861–1865.* Central Falls, R.I., 1876.

Devine, John E. *35th Battalion Virginia Cavalry.* Lynchburg, Va., 1985.

Dew, Charles B. *Ironmaker to the Confederacy: Joseph R. Anderson and the Tredegar Iron Works.* New Haven, Conn., 1966.

Douglas, Henry Kyd. *I Rode with Stonewall.* Chapel Hill, N.C., 1940.

Driver, Robert J., Jr. *First and Second Maryland Cavalry, C.S.A.* Charlottesville, Va., 1999.

———. *The Staunton Artillery—McClanahan's Battery.* Lynchburg, Va., 1988.

———. *1st Virginia Cavalry.* Lynchburg, Va., 1991.

———. *5th Virginia Cavalry.* Lynchburg, Va., 1997.

———. *14th Virginia Cavalry.* Lynchburg, Va., 1988.

———. *52nd Virginia Infantry.* Lynchburg, Va., 1986.

———. *58th Virginia Infantry.* Lynchburg, Va., 1990.

Driver, Robert J., Jr., and Howard, H. E., *2nd Virginia Cavalry.* Lynchburg, Va., 1995.

Early, Jubal Anderson. *Autobiographical Sketch and Narrative of the War Between the States.* Philadelphia, 1912.

Eby, Cecil D., Jr., ed. *A Virginia Yankee in the Civil War: The Diaries of David Hunter Strother.* Chapel Hill, N.C., 1961.

Emerson, Edward W., ed. *Life and Letters of Charles Russell Lowell.* Port Washington, N.Y., 1971.

Evans, Clement A., ed. *Confederate Military History.* 12 vols. Atlanta, Ga., 1899.

Farrar, Samuel Clarke. *The Twenty-Second Pennsylvania Cavalry and the Ringold Battalion, 1861–1865.* Pittsburgh, Pa., 1911.

Fortier, John. *15th Virginia Cavalry.* Lynchburg, Va., 1993.

Foster, Gaines M. *Ghosts of the Confederacy: Defeat, the Lost Cause, and the Emergence of the New South.* New York, 1987.

Freeman, Douglas Southall. *Lee's Lieutenants: A Study in Command.* 3 volumes. New York, 1942–44.

Frye, Dennis E. *2nd Virginia Infantry.* Lynchburg, Va., 1984.

Gallaher, Dewitt Clinton. *A Diary Depicting the Experiences of Dewitt Clinton Gallaher in the War Between the States.* Charleston, S.C., 1961.

Gilmor, Harry. *Four Years in the Saddle.* Baltimore, 1986.

Goldsborough, William W. *The Maryland Line in the Confederate Army, 1861–1865.* Baltimore, 1900.

Gordon, Armistead C. *Staunton, Virginia: Its Past, Present, and Future.* New York, 1890.

Harris, Nelson. *17th Virginia Cavalry.* Lynchburg, Va., 1994.

Hawke, George R. *A History of Waynesboro, Virginia to 1900.* Waynesboro, Va., 1997.

Heatwole, John L. *The Burning: Sheridan in the Shenandoah Valley.* Charlottesville, Va., 1998.

The History of Hebron Presbyterian Church, Staunton, Virginia. Staunton, Va., 1946.

Hewett, Janet B., et al., editors. *Supplement to the Official Records of the Union and Confederate Armies.* 100 vols. Wilmington, N.C., 1994.

Ide, Horace K. *History of the First Vermont Cavalry Volunteers in the War of the Great Rebellion.* Baltimore, 2000.

Illustrated Historical Atlas of Augusta County, Virginia, 1885. Original surveys by Jedediah Hotchkiss. Chicago, 1885.

Johnson, Robert Underwood and C. C. Buel. *Battles and Leaders of the Civil War.* 4 vols. New York, 1887.

Kidd, J. H. *Personal Recollections of a Cavalrymen with Custer's Michigan Brigade in the Civil War.* Grand Rapids, Mich., 1969.

Kleese, Richard B. *Shenandoah County in the Civil War: The Turbulent Years.* Lynchburg, Va., 1992.

———. *23rd Virginia Cavalry.* Lynchburg, Va., 1996.

———. *49th Virginia Infantry.* Appomattox, Va., 2002.

Krick, Robert K. *Conquering the Valley: Stonewall Jackson at Port Republic.* New York, 1996.

———. *Lee's Colonels: A Biographical Register of the Field Officers of the Army of Northern Virginia.* Dayton, Ohio, 1984.

Lewis, Thomas A. *The Shenandoah in Flames: The Valley Campaign of 1864.* Alexandria, Va., 1987.

Lonn, Ella. *Foreigners in the Confederacy.* Chapel Hill, N.C., 1940.

McDonald, Archie P., ed. *Make Me a Map of the Valley, the Civil War Journal of Stonewall Jackson's Topographer, Jedediah Hotchkiss.* Dallas, Tex., 1973.

McDonald, William N. *A History of the Laurel Brigade.* Baltimore, 1907.

McLean, James. *California Sabers: The 2nd Massachusetts Cavalry in the Civil War.* Bloomington, Ind., 2000.

McCue, Elizabeth B. *Staunton, Virginia: A Pictorial History.* Staunton, Va., 1999.

McMurry, Richard M., *Virginia Military Institute Alumni in the Civil War.* Lynchburg, Va., 1999.

MacMaster, Richard K. *Augusta County History 1865–1950.* Staunton, Va., 1964.

Martin, Samuel J. *The Road to Glory: Confederate General Richard S. Ewell.* Indianapolis, Ind., 1991.

May, C. E. *Life Under Four Flags in North River Basin of Virginia.* Verona, Va., 1976.

Miles, Dudley H., ed. *The Photographic History of the Civil War,* Vol. 1–10. New York, 1911.

Miller, William J. *Mapping for Stonewall: The Civil War Service of Jed Hotchkiss.* Washington, D.C., 1993.

Moore, Edward A. *The Story of a Cannoneer under Stonewall Jackson.* Lynchburg, Va., 1910.

Moore, Robert H., II. *The Charlottesville, Lee Lynchburg, and Johnson's Bedford Artillery.* Lynchburg, Va., 1989.

———. *Chew's Ashby, Shoemaker's Lynchburg and the Newtown Artillery.* Lynchburg, Va., 1995.

———. *Graham's Petersburg, Jackson's Kanawha, and Lurty's Roanoke Horse Artillery.* Lynchburg, Va., 1996.

———. *1st and 2nd Stuart Horse Artillery.* Lynchburg, Va., 1999.

Musick, Michael P. *6th Virginia Cavalry.* Lynchburg, Va., 1990.

Myers, Frank M. T*he Comanches: A History of White's Battalion, Virginia Cavalry.* Baltimore, 1871.

Nanzig, Thomas P. *3rd Virginia Cavalry.* Lynchburg, Va., 1989.

Neese, George M. *Three Years in the Confederate Horse Artillery.* Dayton, Ohio, 1988.

O'Ferrall, Charles T. *Forty Years of Active Service: Being Some History of the War Between the Confederacy and the Union and of the Events Leading Up to It.* New York, l904.

Opie, John N. *A Rebel Cavalryman with Lee, Stuart and Jackson.* Chicago, 1899.

Osbourne, Charles C. *Jubal: The Life and Times of General Jubal A. Early, CSA.* Baton Rouge, La., 1992.

Pender, William D. *The General to His Lady: The Civil War Letters of William Dorsey Pender to Fanny Pender.* Ed. by William W. Hassler, Gaithersburg, Md., 1988.

Peyton, J. Lewis. *History of Augusta County.* Bridgewater, Va., 1953.

Pfanz, Donald C. *Richard S. Ewell: A Soldier's Life.* Chapel Hill, N.C., 1998.

Poague, William T. *Gunner with Stonewall.* Edited by Monroe F. Cockrell. Jackson, Tenn., 1957.

Rawling, C. J. *History of the First Regiment Virginia Infantry: Being a Narrative of the Military Movements in the Mountains of Virginia, in the Shenandoah Valley and East of the Blue Ridge During the War of Rebellion, of the First Regiment, Virginia Infantry Volunteers, Three Months' and Three Years' Service.* Philadelphia, 1887.

Reidenbaugh, Lowell. *33rd Virginia Infantry.* Lynchburg, Va., 1987.

Robertson, James I., Jr. *Stonewall Jackson: The Man, The Soldier, The Legend.* New York, 1997.

_____. *The Stonewall Brigade.* Baton Rouge, La., 1963.

Roper, Peter W., *Jedediah Hotchkiss: Rebel Mapmaker and Virginia Businessman.* Shippensburg, Pa., 1992.

Salmon, John S. *The Official Virginia Civil War Battlefield Guide.* Mechanicsburg, Pa., 2001.

Scott, Johnny Lee, *60th Virginia Infantry.* Lynchburg, Va., 1997.

Sellers, Robert L. III, comp. *The Veterans of Thornrose Cemetery,* n.p., 1991.

Sheridan. Philip H. *Personal Memoirs of Philip H. Sheridan, General United States Army.* New York, 1888.

Southern Historical Society Papers. 52 vols. Richmond, Va., 1876–1919.

Starr, Stephen Z. *The Union Cavalry in the Civil War.* 3 vols. Baton Rouge, La., 1981.

Stiles, Kenneth L. *4th Virginia Cavalry.* Lynchburg, Va., 1985.

Strother, David. *Virginia Illustrated: Containing A Visit to the Virginia Canaan and the Adventures of Porte Crayon and his Cousins.* New York, 1871.

Supplement to the Official Records, Part II Record of Events. Wilmington, N.C., 1998.

Tanner, Robert G. *Stonewall in the Valley: Thomas J. "Stonewall" Jackson's Shenandoah Valley Campaign, Spring 1862.* Garden City, New York, 1976.

Tobie, Edward P. *History of the First Maine Cavalry, 1861–1865.* Boston, 1887.

U.S. War Department. *The War of the Rebellion: A Compilation of the Official Records of the Union and Confederate Armies.* 128 vols. Washington, D.C., 1880–1901.

Viola, Herman J. *The Memoirs of Charles Henry Veil: A Soldier's Recollections of the Civil War and the Arizona Territory.* New York, 1993.

Virginia Magazine of History and Biography

Waddell, Joseph. *Annals of Augusta County.* Richmond, Va., 1886.

Wakelyn, Jon L., *Biographical Dictionary of the Confederacy.* Westport, Conn., 1977.

Walker, Aldace F. *The Vermont Brigade in the Shenandoah Valley 1864.* Burlington, Vt., 1869.

Walker, Charles D. *Memorial, Virginia Military Institute.* Philadelphia, 1875.

Wallace, Lee A., Jr. *A Guide to Virginia Military Organizations, 1861–1865.* Lynchburg, Va., 1986.

———. *5th Virginia Infantry.* Lynchburg, Va., 1988.

Warner, Ezra J. *Generals in Blue: Lives of the Union Commanders.* Baton Rouge, La., 1964.

———. *Generals in Gray: Lives of the Confederate Commanders.* Baton Rouge, La., 1959.

———. *5th Virginia Infantry.* Lynchburg, Va., 1988.

Wayland, John W. *A History of Rockingham County, Virginia.* Dayton, Va., 1912.

———. *A History of Shenandoah County, Virginia.* Strasburg, Va., 1927.

———. *Stonewall Jackson's Way.* Verona, Va., 1969.

Weaver, Jeffrey C. *22nd Virginia Cavalry.* Lynchburg, Va., 1991.

Wert, Jeffrey D. *From Winchester to Cedar Creek: The Shenandoah Campaign of 1864.* Carlisle, Pa. 1987.

Wilson, Howard McKnight. *The Tinkling Spring, Headwater of Freedom: A Study of the Church and Her People, 1732–1952.* Fishersville, Va., 1954.

Wise, Jennings Cropper, *The Long Arm of Lee.* Richmond, Va., 1988.

Worsham, John H. *One of Jackson's Foot Cavalry.* New York, 1912.

Index

About the Author

A native of Page County, Virginia, Robert H. Moore II completed most of his undergraduate work at East Carolina University and received his Bachelor of Science degree in Liberal Studies from Excelsior College in 1995. He is currently in the process of completing his M.A. in History at Old Dominion University. A ten-year veteran of the submarine force of the United States Navy, Robert has written seven books for the Virginia Regimental History Series and an eighth book about Civil War sites in Luray and Page County. This book is his ninth and examines Civil War sites in Staunton, Waynesboro, and Augusta County. He has also written extensively for magazines such as *Civil War Times Illustrated*, *Blue and Gray Magazine*, and *America's Civil War*. For the past six years, Robert has also maintained the "Heritage and Heraldry" newspaper column *(Page News and Courier)* featuring Page County history and genealogy. Robert also serves on the History Committee for Virginia Civil War Trails and the Education and Interpretation Committee of the Shenandoah Valley Battlefields Foundation. A former chairman of the Page County Civil War Commission, Robert has played a role in securing funding for twelve Virginia Civil War Trails markers in Page County and has written texts for signs throughout the Shenandoah Valley. He is presently the Commander of the 4th Brigade, Virginia Division, Sons of Confederate Veterans and is also Commander of the Summers-Koontz Camp No. 490, Sons of Confederate Veterans, in Luray. He currently resides with his family in Augusta County.